Practical Phonetics

Practical Phonetics

J. C. Wells PhD
Lecturer in Phonetics, University College, London

and **Greta Colson**
Principal Lecturer in charge of Voice, New College of Speech and Drama

Pitman Publishing

First published 1971

SIR ISAAC PITMAN AND SONS LTD
Pitman House, Parker Street, Kingsway, London WC2B 5PB
P.O. Box 6038, Portal Street, Nairobi, Kenya
SIR ISAAC PITMAN (AUST.) PTY LTD
Pitman House, 158 Bouverie Street, Carlton, Victoria 3053, Australia
PITMAN PUBLISHING COMPANY S.A. LTD
P.O. Box 11231, Johannesburg, S. Africa
PITMAN PUBLISHING CORPORATION
6 East 43rd Street, New York, N.Y. 10017, U.S.A.
SIR ISAAC PITMAN (CANADA) LTD
495 Wellington Street West, Toronto 135, Canada
THE COPP CLARK PUBLISHING COMPANY
517 Wellington Street West, Toronto 135, Canada

ISBN: 0 273 43949 9

Made in Great Britain at the Pitman Press, Bath
G1—(G.3573: 15)

Preface

This book has been written as an easy introduction to phonetics, the study of pronunciation. It is intended for those whose mother tongue is English—and particularly for those who may wrongly have imagined phonetics to be a dull, dry, or difficult subject. It aims to hold the student's interest, while leading him steadily onward. Plenty of practical examples and exercises are provided, although teachers may of course wish to supplement these with further material.

The book covers the basic elements of general phonetics and English phonetics. A student who has mastered its contents will be well on the way to success in the International Phonetic Association's Certificate examination or the phonetics paper of such examinations as that for the Licentiate Diploma of the College of Speech Therapists. We hope the book will prove of value to many students of English language, speech therapy, linguistics, speech and drama, and allied subjects.

Acknowledgements

The authors' thanks are due for permission to reproduce the following passages:

Page 33. From *Three Men in a Boat* by Jerome K. Jerome, published by J. M. Dent & Sons Ltd.

Pages 46 and 88. "Cri Zok," "Bombast" and "Tan tandinanan" by Bob Cobbing.

Page 56. "The Rise and Fall of the River Mersey" from *A Plea for Mersey* by Peter Molony, published by Gallery Press.

Pages 58–9. From the book *The House at Pooh Corner* by A. A. Milne, published by Methuen & Co. Ltd. (Copyright 1928 in the United States and Canada by E. P. Dutton & Co. Inc. Renewal 1956 by A. A. Milne.)

Page 65. From *The Crane Bag* by Robert Graves. Published by Cassell & Co. Ltd.

Pages 69, 90, 96. From the *Sunday Express*.

Pages, 70, 72, 75, 79, 102. From the *Observer*.

Page 74. From *Under Milk Wood* by Dylan Thomas, by permission of J. M. Dent & Sons Ltd. and the Trustees for the copyright of the late Dylan Thomas. (Copyright in the United States 1954 by New Directions Publishing Corporation.)

The chart on pages viii–ix is reproduced by permission of the International Phonetic Association.

Contents

THE INTERNATIONAL PHONETIC ALPHABET.
(Revised to 1951.)

CONSONANTS

	Bi-labial	Labio-dental	Dental and Alveolar	Retroflex	Palato-alveolar	Alveolo-palatal	Palatal	Velar	Uvular	Pharyngal	Glottal
Plosive	p b		t d	ʈ ɖ			c ɟ	k g	q ɢ		ʔ
Nasal	m	ɱ	n	ɳ			ɲ	ŋ	N		
Lateral Fricative			ɬ ɮ								
Lateral Non-fricative			l	l			ʎ				
Rolled			r						R		
Flapped			ɾ	ɽ					ʀ		
Fricative	ɸ β	f v	θ ð | s z | ɹ	ʂ ʐ	ʃ ʒ	ɕ ʑ	ç ʝ	x ɣ	χ ʁ	ħ ʕ	h ɦ
Frictionless Continuants and Semi-vowels	w ɥ	ʋ	ɹ				j (ɥ)	(w)	ʁ		

VOWELS

	Front	Central	Back
Close	i y	ɨ ʉ	ɯ u
Half-close	(y ø u)	ə	ɤ o
Half-open	(ø o)	e	ʌ ɔ
Half-open	(œ ɔ)	œ ɜ	ʌ ɔ
Open	(ɒ)	æ	ɑ ɒ

(Secondary articulations are shown by symbols in brackets.)

OTHER SOUNDS.—Palatalized consonants: ţ, ḑ, etc.; palatalized ʃ, ȝ: ᶘ, ᶚ. Velarized or pharyngalized consonants: ɫ, d̴, z̴, etc. Ejective consonants (with simultaneous glottal stop): p', t', etc. Implosive voiced consonants: ɓ, ɗ, etc. r fricative trill. σ, ʒ (labialized θ, ð, or s, z). ʮ, ʯ (labialized ʃ, ȝ). ʇ, ʗ, ʖ (clicks, Zulu c, q, x). l (a sound between r and l). ɳ Japanese syllabic nasal. ꜰ (combination of x and ʃ). ʍ (voiceless w). ɿ, ʮ, ɷ (lowered varieties of i, y, u). з (a variety of ə). ɵ (a vowel between ø and o).

Affricates are normally represented by groups of two consonants (ts, tʃ, dȝ, etc.), but, when necessary, ligatures are used (ʦ, ʧ, ʤ etc.), or the marks ⌒ or ‿ (t͡s or t͜s, etc.). ‿ also denote synchronic articulation (m͡ŋ = simultaneous m and ŋ). c, ɟ may occasionally be used in place of tʃ, dȝ, and ʒ, ᴣ for ts, dz. Aspirated plosives: ph, th, etc. r-coloured vowels: eɹ, aɹ, ɑɹ, etc., or eʵ, aʵ, ɔʵ, etc., or ȩ, a̧, ɔ̧, etc.; r-coloured ə : əɹ or əʵ or ɹ or ɚ, or ɚ.

LENGTH, STRESS, PITCH.— : (full length). · (half length). ˈ (stress, placed at beginning of the stressed syllable). ˌ (secondary stress). ˉ (high level pitch); ˍ (low level); ˊ (high rising); ˏ (low rising); ˋ (high falling); ˎ (low falling); ˅ (rise-fall); ˄ (fall-rise).

MODIFIERS.— ˜ nasality. ˳ breath (l̥ = breathed l). ˬ voice (ṣ = z). ˑ slight aspiration following p, t, etc. ˳ labialization (n̫ = labialized n). ̪ dental articulation (t̪ = dental t). ˙ palatalization (ż = ȝ). ˏ specially close vowel (ẹ = a very close e). ˎ specially open vowel (e̩ = a rather open e). ⊢ tongue raised (e̗ or e̝ = ẹ). ⊣ tongue lowered (e̞ or e̠ = e̩). + tongue advanced (u̟ or u̟ = an advanced u, ṭ = t̪). ˗ or ⊣ tongue retracted (i̠ or i̱ = ɨ, ṱ = alveolar t). ˷ lips more rounded. ˂ lips more spread. Central vowels: ï (= ɨ), ü (= ʉ), ë (= ə), ö (= ө), ɛ̈, ɔ̈. ˎ (e.g. n̩) syllabic consonant. ˋ consonantal vowel. ʃ variety of ʃ resembling s, etc.

1   Air-streams

Phonetics is the study and description of pronunciation. It is concerned with WHAT we pronounce and HOW we pronounce it. In order to learn how we make speech sounds, we shall study the workings of the various organs of speech. In order to get a better idea of what we pronounce (which may be by no means what we think we pronounce), we shall make use of special phonetic symbols, which enable us to refer to sounds independently of spelling.

For the practical work in this course, a teacher is needed. The teacher should give dictation for ear-training purposes and check the student's production of unfamiliar sounds and sound sequences.

For us to make any sound with our organs of speech, air has to be set in motion. If no air moves, no sound results. In ordinary speech, air is set in motion from the lungs. It then passes through the throat and the mouth and/or nose, and so into the outer air. Breath enters and leaves the body in accordance with the alternate increase and decrease in the size of the chest, and hence in the size of the lungs (since the lungs expand and contract according to the size of the chest). These changes in the size of the chest are brought about by alternate contraction and relaxation of the muscles. The size of the chest is increased laterally by the contraction of the external intercostal muscles and vertically by the contraction of the diaphragm.

After the air-stream has left the lungs it may be modified in various ways before passing out through the mouth or nose.

Make a good long f sound. Feel the movement of the air involved.

The sound f is articulated by means of contact between the lower lip and the upper teeth. Distinguish between this ARTICULATION (the nature of the barrier to the air-stream) and the AIR-STREAM MECHANISM (the way the air-stream is set in motion—also called the INITIATION).

A sort of f sound can also be made while sucking breath into the lungs. Try this.

1

The air-stream mechanism in ordinary speech is termed PULMONIC EGRES-SIVE. It is pulmonic, because the air is set in motion in the lungs; it is egressive, because the direction of the movement is outwards. But a pulmonic air-stream can move in either direction, outwards or inwards. Inflowing, it is called INGRESSIVE; outflowing, it is EGRESSIVE. Although ingressive sounds are easy to make, they rarely occur in speech.

> Make s first egressively, then ingressively. Alternate them, first one then the other. Do the same for ɑ (i.e. an *ah*-sound), for t and for b. Try talking with an ingressive air-stream—try phrases like *Good morning, What do you think? Would you excuse me, please?* Try counting, from one to ten and further, as far as you can get on one ingressive breath. Compare counting on an egressive breath.

We can only talk for very short stretches with an ingressive air-stream. With an ordinary egressive air-stream, on the other hand, we can talk for twenty seconds or more in one breath. This is because we have had much more practice at fine control of the egressive breath.

An ingressive air-stream is sometimes used to make speech sounds. *Yes* may be said ingressively sometimes; there is also an ingressive ejaculation rather like *sh!* used as a response to pain.

The air-streams we have dealt with so far have been pulmonic. A familiar but non-pulmonic air-stream is that used to make CLICKS. These are sounds made entirely within the mouth, not using the lungs. Their air-stream mechanism is ORAL.

> Make the sound usually written as *tut-tut*. (Its phonetic symbol is ʇ.) Can you make it between vowel sounds?

The air flows inwards in the *tut-tut* click, so we say it has an ORAL INGRES-SIVE air-stream. The air is sucked into the mouth by the muscular action of the tongue against the roof of the mouth—the tongue acts rather like a rubber sucker pulling against a ceiling.

> If the tongue is released at the side instead of at the tip we get another click, the *gee-up!* click used to encourage horses (phonetic symbol ʖ). It too has an oral ingressive air-stream.

It is also possible to make sounds with an ORAL EGRESSIVE air-stream: that is, an air-stream initiated solely inside the mouth, not using the lungs or throat—but flowing outwards.

> Experiment with oral egressive air-streams. One sound of this type is associated with removing food from between the teeth. Another is known colloquially as a "raspberry."

2

It is possible to make a pulmonic egressive air-stream sound, namely an *ng*-sound as in *sing* (phonetic symbol ŋ) at the same time as any click. The result is called a nasalized click.

> Try the nasalized clicks corresponding to the ʇ and ʖ already practised. The nasalized ʇ is sometimes used in English as a kind of interjection to show contempt or disparagement.
> Can you make a nasalized "raspberry"?

In fact all sounds made with the oral air-stream mechanism require a closure between the back of the tongue and the soft palate, so clicks can be made in the middle of a **g** or **k** as well as an **ŋ**.

A third pair of air-stream mechanisms involve holding the vocal folds together and using the air above them in the throat (pharynx). If a PHARYN-GEAL air-stream made like this is egressive, the result is an EJECTIVE consonant. The air is compressed behind its articulation by the raising of the larynx, which acts like a pump.

> Take a breath and hold it. While still holding the breath, articulate **p, t, k**, or any other consonant.

Some people use ejectives in English when words ending in **p, t, k**, or **tʃ** (a *ch*-sound) come at the ends of sentences.

> Say the following words with ejective consonants at the end: *pick, plate, stamp, bench.*

Sounds made with an ingressive pharyngeal air-stream are called IMPLOSIVE. The necessary suction is made by holding the vocal folds closed and lowering the larynx sharply.

> Try making implosive **p, t, k, tʃ**, etc.

If, during an implosive, a little lung air trickles through the vocal folds with a "straining" noise, the result is a VOICED IMPLOSIVE. Sounds of this type occur in several African languages.

> Try and make implosive sounds corresponding to **b, d, g** (phonetic symbols: **ɓ, ɗ, ɠ**).

We have now covered six different air-stream mechanisms. We can tabulate them as follows—

3

PULMONIC	{egressive	ordinary speech
	ingressive	in-breathing speech
PHARYNGEAL	{egressive	ejective
	ingressive	implosive
ORAL	{egressive	reverse click
	ingressive	click

Note: some phoneticians use the terms GLOTTALIC and VELARIC instead of PHARYNGEAL and ORAL respectively.

It is also possible to use a belch (burp) as an air-stream for speech. People who have had their larynxes removed for surgical reasons learn to do this. Since the air involved is expelled from the oesophagus, we call this the OESOPHAGEAL egressive air-mechanism.

If you care to, try talking with an oesophageal air-stream. To begin with, limit yourself to one syllable per burp.

There is no need to worry if you find it difficult to produce sounds made with non-pulmonic air-streams.

2 Transcription

By systematic practice in listening to sounds one can greatly improve one's ability to recognize and distinguish different speech sounds. Such practice is known as EAR-TRAINING. It is best done by taking dictation from someone familiar with the phonetic material to be studied.

Another form of practice very useful in increasing one's phonetic awareness is making transcriptions—writing down in phonetic symbols the way a passage of English would be pronounced. Doing this, one has to concentrate on SOUNDS and free one's ideas from the influence (often misleading) of ordinary SPELLING.

For both these purposes we represent sounds by PHONETIC SYMBOLS, some of which are ordinary letters used in a consistent and specified way, and some of which are new letter shapes. They help us to note down and refer to sounds independently of spelling. We can begin with five vowel-sounds and three consonant-sounds, as follows—

SYMBOLS	KEYWORD
i	b*ea*t
ɑ	f*a*ther
u	m*oo*n
ɔ	b*ough*t
3	b*ir*d
p	*pip*
t	*t*augh*t*
k	*c*oo*k*

We can use these symbols to transcribe various English words—

pit	*peat*
kɔk	*cork*
tu	*too, two*

Looking at the last example, note how English spelling obscures the fact that *two* and *too* are pronounced identically. (Sometimes *to* is pronounced **tu** as well.)

Transcribe the following words—
tea, paw, purr, park, coo

Write down the following words (or similar ones) from dictation. Put down both ordinary spelling and phonetic symbols—

key	**ki**
tar, ta	**tɑ**
curt	**kɜt**
talk	**tɔk**
peat	**pit**

Obviously, not everyone has exactly the same pronuncibtion of English. For some accents we should need to use a partly different set of symbols, or use them in different ways. The pronunciation used in this book is an educated pronunciation of England—a kind which does not have any regional characteristics. But the transcription used for this SOUTHERN BRITISH STANDARD (also called RECEIVED PRONUNCIATION or RP) will serve with very little modification for any educated accent of England and Wales, Australia, New Zealand, or South Africa. For the English heard in America, Scotland, Ireland, and the West Indies we might need a rather different type of transcription.

Notice that in Southern British Standard pronunciation there is no **r**-sound corresponding to the *r* in words such as *park*, *curt*, *cork*. Accordingly we transcribe them **pɑk, kɜt, kɔk**.

Say these words over to yourself, noticing whether you actually pronounce an **r**-sound. If you don't, try them for contrast with an **r**, the way they are pronounced in the West Country, Scotland, Ireland, or America—

pɑrk kɜrt kɔrk

If on the other hand you usually pronounce these words with an **r**-sound, try them without—

pɑk kɜt kɔk

The following NONSENSE WORDS (or similar ones) should be written down in phonetic symbols only, from dictation. They give practice in recognizing sounds when no help can be had from the meaning—

kɜp	**tɑp**	**tɜt**	**put**
kik	**pɔp**	**kit**	**tuk**

EXERCISES

1. Say aloud the words represented by the following phonetic transcription—

pɑk	**tɜk**	**kup**	**kɔt**	**it**
ɑk	**pɑt**	**tik**	**kɑt**	**pɔt**

2. Transcribe the following words—
pa, paw, peak, kirk, Pooh, purr, talk, pert, ought, car.

3. How many differently spelt words are pronounced **kɔt**? **pɔ**? **pɑ**? In how many different ways can the sound **k** be represented in ordinary spelling? The sound **i**? The sound **ɔ**?

3　The Vocal Folds

EAR-TRAINING

pɜtuk
tɔpit
kɑkɑkt
pikput

The vocal folds (or vocal cords, or vocal lips) lie in the larynx, behind the adam's apple. They are like elastic lips, running fore-and-aft across the windpipe. If they come firmly together, they block the passage of air: this is what we call "holding the breath," and is how we make the sound known as the glottal plosive or glottal stop. If they lie open and apart, they allow the outgoing air a free passage. But one of their most important functions is producing voice.

Say **fff** (a long f-sound), and then **vvv** (a long v-sound). Feel the difference between them as you repeat them and alternate them.

These two sounds, **f** and **v**, have the same air-stream mechanism and the same articulation. The difference between them lies in the VOICING of **v**.

Voicing is due to the rapid vibration of the vocal folds: that is, they open and shut repeatedly. For a man's middle note the vibration may be 130 to 140 times a second; for higher notes the rate of vibration is greater, and for lower notes less.

Experiment with further pairs of voiceless and voiced sounds. Say **sss**, then **zzz**. Say an **m**-sound (which is voiced), and then try its voiceless counterpart **m̥m̥m̥**.

Similarly say **ɑɑɑ** and then voiceless **ɑ̥ɑ̥ɑ̥**. Alternate quickly **fvfvfv, szszsz, m̥mm̥mm̥m, ɑ̥ɑɑ̥ɑɑ̥ɑ**.

There are several ways of testing whether a sound is voiced or voiceless.

1. Place the thumb and forefinger gently on the outside of the larynx and feel the vibration present during voiced sounds.

2. Put your hands over your ears and feel the loud buzzing which fills the head during voiced sounds.

8

Other ways involve the use of apparatus (stethoscope, oscilloscope, speech spectrograph).

Decide whether the following sounds are voiced or voiceless: **h w n.**

Practise control over voicing, until you can switch it on or off at will.

Say **n ṇ n ṇ**. (The symbol ₀ underneath a letter shows voicelessness.) Then try **ŋ** on its own and between vowel-sounds.

Try **mṃmṃmṃ** and **lḷlḷlḷ**. Try devoicing any other voiced sounds you can make—e.g. a rolled **r**-sound, uvular or lingual. (If you can make a uvular roll and devoice it, try whistling at the same time—like a referee's whistle.)

In doing these exercises you are extending the range of sounds you can make.

The GLOTTIS is the space between the vocal folds. The term "voiced" and the term "voiceless" thus refer to different states of the glottis. If the glottis is vibrating, a voiced sound results: if the glottis is wide open, a voiceless sound results. If the glottis is open but not very wide open, the air can only pass through with a certain amount of difficulty, and WHISPER is heard.

Make the voiced sound **ɑ** and then the corresponding whispered and voiceless sounds.

By closing the glottis we hold the breath and make a glottal plosive (phonetic symbol **ʔ**).

Alternate vowel-sound and glottal plosive, thus **ɑʔɑʔɑʔ**.

We also close the glottis for other, physiological, reasons—when lifting something heavy, for example.

Try this way of testing whether the glottis is open or closed. 1. Make an **h**-sound, and meanwhile flick the neck just above the larynx with the forefinger. A dullish sound is heard. 2. Do the same thing while holding your breath, i.e. making a glottal plosive. A louder and more hollow sound is now produced by flicking, and its pitch can be varied by changing the position of the tongue, rounding the lips, etc.

Note three new phonetic symbols for vowel-sounds—

ɪ	b*i*t
ɛ	b*e*t
æ	b*a*t

9

And some symbols for consonants, all familiar—

b	*baby*
d	*dandy*
g	*giggle*
f	*fifty*
v	*vivid*
s	*cease* (note that the sound is the same, though the spelling is different)
z	*zones* (the same remark applies)
r	*red*
l	*lead*
w	*witch*
h	*hothouse*
m	*murmur*
n	*nanny*

Transcribe, or write in phonetic symbols from the teacher's dictation, the following words—

bee, gawp, do, bird, guard, kit, tan, ten, knit, ban, fend, web.

What words are represented by the following transcriptions?

bæg mɛn gæs pis fit kɔs væn fɜst lɪm wɔt huf kɑf rud vɜb vɛst

Now try some two-syllable words—

mɪnɪt pɜmɪt kɑpɪt ænɛks brɔdkɑst

Where the spelling is *c* the sound may be either **k** or **s**. Transcribe the following, being careful never to write **c**, only **k** or **s** as appropriate.

cat, call, calm, cent, cigar, panic, pencil, access.

Note how misleading the ordinary spelling may be: *seas, sees* and *seize* are all pronounced **siz**.

Words pronounced the same but spelt differently are called HOMOPHONES. So *troupe* and *troop* are homophones, as are *meat* and *meet*. The phonetic transcriptions of a word and its homophone are identical: **trup, mit**. (Such pairs can also be termed, less specifically, HOMONYMS.)

How are *sent, scent,* and *cent* transcribed?

Different ways of pronouncing English lead to the existence of different sets of homophones. In Southern British Standard *carve* and *calve* are homophones, since both are pronounced kʌv; in other accents the two words may be distinguished. Similarly *cause* and *cores*, SBS kɔz: these are distinguished not only by r-pronouncers but also by many Londoners.

Test the following pairs by saying them aloud. Some are homophones for everybody, some only in certain accents.

feet—feat	*kernel—colonel*
ant—aunt	*tear* (rip)—*tear* (weeping)
pair—pear—pare	*faint—feint*
rows—roes—rose	*sure—shore*
plaice—place	*slow—sloe*
hare—hair	*which—witch*

Transcribe from dictation—

ist ɛnd—izd ɛnd
lɛt mi—lɛd mi
hæt pɪn—hæd bɪn
stɑvd—stɑft

4 Place of Articulation

EAR-TRAINING

Transcribe from dictation—

bɪg bɛn	pɪk tɛn
brɛd bɪn	sit bɛlt
tu wiks liv	fɔ wæks livz

We must now consider not so much how a sound is articulated as where it is articulated. In all sounds we shall be dealing with here, the air-stream passes from the lungs through the trachea (windpipe) and larynx into the mouth and/or nose.

Study the diagram of the organs of speech (page 13).

To make **p**, the lips are pressed together so as to prevent the air-stream from escaping from the mouth. (As we shall see later, the air cannot pass out through the nose, because the soft palate is raised.) The air comes into the mouth but is blocked behind the BILABIAL barrier. **b** and **m** are also bilabial sounds, since they too are articulated with a barrier formed by the two closed lips.

Say **p**, **b**, and **m** several times each, getting the feeling of their articulation. For variation, try making them in an **f** position—with the barrier formed by the lower lip and the upper teeth instead. Say *happy*, *baby*, *Mummy* while laughing!

f and **v** are made with the lower lip and upper teeth and are accordingly termed LABIO-DENTAL.

You can also make rather similar sounds to **p**, **b**, etc., by placing the tongue against the upper lip. Try saying *happy* in this way. But as far as we know no language uses these LINGUO-LABIAL sounds.

We have two sounds in English made by placing the tongue tip against the backs of the upper teeth (sometimes by putting it further forward, between the teeth). They are the *th*-sounds: the voiceless one, **θ**, as in *thick*,

12

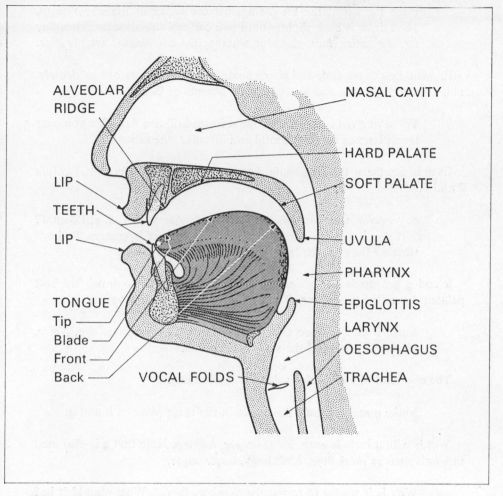

Diagrammatic view of a section through nose, mouth and neck, showing the organs of speech

thought, thirteenth, and the voiced one, **ð**, as in *this, though, other.* They are termed DENTAL.

> Read the words transcribed as follows: **θɔt, ðæt, ðɛn, hɑθ.** Transcribe: *wreath, thirst, these, earth.* How do different members of the class pronounce *with*?

t, d, n, l, s, and **z** are made by placing the tip or blade of the tongue against the gum just behind the upper teeth. This ridge of gum is called the alveolar ridge, and the sounds articulated there are termed ALVEOLAR.

13

Place the tip of the tongue against the backs of the upper teeth. Then draw it back slightly until you can feel the alveolar ridge. Say *tar*, *den*, *seize*, *loot*, checking whether the consonants are alveolar.

In some languages **t**, **d**, and **n** are made not as alveolars but as dentals. This is true of French, and also of certain accents of English.

Try saying *ten* with dental **t** and **n** instead of alveolar. Can you hear the difference between dental and alveolar when dictated?

Even in Southern British Standard **t**, **d**, **n**, and **l** are usually dental before **θ** and **ð**.

Say *wealth*, *width*, *eighth*, *tenth*, *add this*. Are your **t**, **d**, **n**, **l** dental? If you have access to native speakers of other languages, find out whether they use dental or alveolar sounds (or both).

k and **g** are made by raising the back of the tongue to touch the soft palate (also called the VELUM). Their place of articulation is VELAR.

Make **k** and **g** alone and in words such as *car*, *guess*, *dog*, *baker*, *bigger*. Try and feel the velar articulation.

The *ng*-sound of *sing* is also velar. Its symbol is **ŋ**.

Make **ŋ** and feel how it is made in the same place as **k** and **g**.

Words with **ŋ** include *rung*, *hang*, *banger*, *longing*. Note that **ŋ** is also used in words such as *think* **θɪŋk**, *bank* **bæŋk**, *anger* **æŋgə**.

Why is it wrong to transcribe *thank* as **θæŋk**? What should it be?

In some accents of the Midlands and North, **ŋ** never occurs by itself but only with a following **k** or **g**. So *singing* may be said as **sɪŋgɪŋg** rather than the standard **sɪŋɪŋ**.

Try out those two ways of saying *singing*. Other possibilities are **sɪŋɪŋg**, **sɪŋgɪŋ**. Find out which each member of the class commonly uses.
Transcribe your pronunciation of the word *dinghy* (a small boat). Some say it with **ŋg** after the first vowel, others with just **ŋ**. Similar variations occur with *English* and *language*: poll the class or your friends.

In the word *morning* mɔnɪŋ, the m is bilabial, the n alveolar, and the ŋ velar.

Take the words *packet* pækɪt, *topic* tɒpɪk, *lacking* lækɪŋ, *band* bænd. Write down the place of articulation of each sound.

Here are three new symbols for vowel sounds—

ʌ   *cup, love*
ʊ   *good, put*
ɒ   *hot* (this symbol is ɑ upside down).

Transcribe: *look, suck, dog, guard, vast, knot, could, cud, cod, card, cad.*
Read: mɑk, mɒk, mʌk, bʊk, mæd, mʌd, wɜd, wɛd, stɒk, stɔk, stæk, stɑk.

Transcribe the words *wasp, clasp, asp.*

In Southern British Standard *wasp* is wɒsp, *clasp* is klɑsp and *asp* is æsp. Notice how the same spelling with *a* corresponds to three different vowel-sounds. In the Midlands and North of England, however, *clasp* may rhyme with *asp*.

There are many words where social or personal differences of pronunciation are found. Thus *plastic* may be plæstɪk or plɑstɪk—both pronunciations are acceptable in Southern British Standard. So also *drastic* as dræstɪk or drɑstɪk, and *elastic* as ɪlæstɪk or ɪlɑstɪk.

Conduct a poll along the class or your friends to find out which pronunciation is commoner. What about *gymnastic*? And *spastic*? And is *graph* more commonly græf or grɑf?

Often such differences are regional. So *past* is pɑst in SBS and in the South of England, but pæst in the North (and in America). The number *one*, usually wʌn, is often wɒn in the Midlands and North.

15

5 More Transcription

REVISION EAR-TRAINING
bɪgmɪŋ
fɒkshʌnt
ʌŋkɒmən
kʊkbʊk
kʌm ɒn ʌp
bi ʌpstændɪŋ ənd drɪŋk
ɒnwəd ənd ʌpwəd

Refer now to the table of phonetic symbols for transcribing English (page 17). We have already dealt with most of the consonant symbols; note the following new ones—

ʃ   *sh*eep
ʒ   plea*s*ure, vi*s*ion
tʃ   *ch*ur*ch*
dʒ   *j*u*dg*e
j   *y*et

Be careful over the last two—the phonetic symbol **j** has a different meaning from the *j* of English spelling.

Transcribe—
sheet, ash, rouge, chest, catch, jet, edge, charge, young, you.

But the sound **j** is not always spelt *y*. Study the following—

few   fju
cute   kjut
tune   tjun
new   nju
amuse   əmjuz

Compare *moo* **mu** with *mew* **mju**.
Transcribe the following—
due, duke, rebuke, argue, accuse, loose, rude, view, blue, shoe.

16

PHONETIC SYMBOLS FOR TRANSCRIBING ENGLISH

1	i	bead	/bid/	p	pip	/pɪp/
2	ɪ	bid	/bɪd/	b	barb	/bɑb/
3	ɛ	bed	/bɛd/	t	tact, tacked	/tækt/
4	æ	bad	/bæd/	d	dared	/dɛəd/
5	ɑ	card	/kɑd/	k	cake	/keɪk/
6	ɒ	cod	/kɒd/	g	gargle	/gɑgl̩/
7	ɔ	caught, court	/kɔt/	tʃ	church	/tʃɜtʃ/
8	ʊ	good	/gʊd/	dʒ	judge	/dʒʌdʒ/
9	u	food	/fud/	f	fearful	/fɪəfl̩/
10	ʌ	bud	/bʌd/	v	vivid	/vɪvɪd/
11	ɜ	bird	/bɜd/	θ	thirteenth	/θɜtinθ/

		announcer	/ənaʊnsə/	ð	the brother	/ðə brʌðə/
12	ə	laboured	/leɪbəd/	s	cease	/sis/
		vanilla	/vənɪlə/	z	zones	/zəʊnz/
13	eɪ	may	/meɪ/	ʃ	sheepish	/ʃipɪʃ/
14	əʊ	mow	/məʊ/	ʒ	treasure	/trɛʒə/
15	aɪ	high	/haɪ/	h	hothouse	/hɒthaʊs/
16	aʊ	how	/haʊ/	m	murmur	/mɜmə/
17	ɒɪ	boy	/bɒɪ/	n	nanny	/nænɪ/
18	ɪə	rear	/rɪə/	ŋ	fingering	/fɪŋgərɪŋ/
19	ɛə	rare	/rɛə/	l	lull	/lʌl/
20	ʊə	Ruhr	/rʊə/	r	reared	/rɪəd/
—	l̩	battle	/bætl̩/	j	use, yews	/juz/
—	n̩	fatten	/fætn̩/	w	witch	/wɪtʃ/

Note: Some people prefer to use the letter ɩ rather than ɪ and ᴏ rather than ʊ. This affects the symbolization of vowels 2, 8, 13–18, and 20.

The symbol ʔ (glottal stop) should not be used in ordinary (phonemic) transcription of English.

The following extra symbols which may be needed are discussed in Chapter 6—

ɒə	*pores*	/pɒəz/	(if different from *pause* or *paws*)
aə	*fire*	/faə/	
ɑə	*power*	/pɑə/	
hw	*whine*	/hwaɪn/	(if different from *wine*)

Conduct a poll for *suit*—do more people say **sjut** or **sut**? Does it depend on where they come from? Do the same for *lewd*, **ljud** or **lud**, and *assume*, **əsjum** or **əsum**.

Where do people come from who say **nu** for *new*? List other words where such people have **u** against the SBS **ju**.

We have already dealt with the vowels numbered 1 to 11. Number 12, **ə**, is very common in unstressed syllables and can be spelt in a large number of different ways.

Read—

bɛtə sæləd əgri bɪgə kəlɛkt kəmɑndmənt

Note how the prefix *con-* is usually pronounced **kɒn** when stressed (**kɒnsət, kɒntækt**), but **kən** when unstressed (**kənsɪdə, kəntɪnju**). This does not apply in Northern accents, where it may always be **kɒn**—observe in this connection that the highest-prestige pronunciation is not always the one that follows the spelling most closely.

The prefix *ex-* may be **ɪks, ɛks,** or **əks** when unstressed as in *except, explain, extend*. Which pronunciation is commonest? Are all three SBS, or is one of them regional? Are *except* and *accept* homonyms?

Distinguish carefully between number 11, **ɜ**, and number 12, **ə**. Both occur in the words *further* **fɜðə**, *occur* **əkɜ** (rarely **əʊkɜ, ɒkɜ**), *surplus* **sɜpləs**, *murderers* **mɜdərəz**. The word *commerce* is usually pronounced **kɒmɜs**, so that it does not rhyme with *Thomas* **tɒməs**.

Transcribe—
urban, murmurs, Persia, versus, disturb, purpose, astir, refer, sermon.

It may be more difficult for some students to grasp the difference between 12, **ə**, and number 10, **ʌ**. Indeed, in transcribing Midlands, Northern, or many American accents we should not be justified in distinguishing them at all. But speakers of SBS and those from the South usually make quite a clear difference between the two vowel sounds. Study the following examples—

summer	**sʌmə**
other	**ʌðə**
thorough	**θʌrə**
above	**əbʌv**

The word *income* may have either **ʌ** or **ə** in its second syllable, and these are alternative pronunciations on a par with **drɑstɪk** versus **dræstɪk** and the like. Compare also *humdrum* hʌmdrʌm versus *conundrum* kənʌndrəm, *unending* ʌnɛndɪŋ versus *an ending* ən ɛndɪŋ.

Transcribe—
butter, supper, another, coloured, among, brothers, suggest, collect, succeed, pick-up.

The CLOSING DIPHTHONGS, numbers 13 to 17, should offer no difficulty. The two letters making the symbol in each case suggest, but do not precisely specify, the beginning and end of the diphthongal glide used. So the starting-point of əʊ, for example, may be just like ə; but it may also sound rather different, depending on regional, social, and personal factors.

Transcribe, or write from dictation—
cry, crow, die, day, dough, now, know, nigh, neigh, toy, late, light, lout, voice, vice, mouse, mace, coat, kite, bake.

The CENTRING DIPHTHONGS, numbers 18 to 20, may present more difficulty. In words like *beard, fear*, speakers of SBS use diphthong number 18, ɪə, thus bɪəd, fɪə. In other accents of English, however, the sequences iə, ir, or ɪr may be used. Note the following for SBS—

nearer	nɪərə
hero	hɪərəʊ
really	rɪəlɪ
idea	aɪdɪə

Does *nearly* rhyme with *really*? Poll several people, and draw conclusions about how their pronunciation of *really* and *nearly* should be transcribed.

Many Americans rhyme *mirror* and *nearer*. How does this come about? Would you expect such speakers to distinguish in pronunciation between *serious* and *Sirius*?

Transcribe the following in SBS—
beer, clearer, dearest, Vera, fearing.

Somewhat similar considerations apply to ɛə. Note that ɛə and ɜ are not distinguished in the west of the North of England (e.g. Liverpool). So *stir* (SBS stɜ) and *stair, stare* (SBS stɛə) are homonyms for some people.

19

Note the following—

fair	fɛə
sharing	ʃɛərɪŋ
Mary	mɛərɪ
Sarah	sɛərə

Transcribe—
mare, mayor, glare, bearing, heiress, squarest, dairy, fairing, bareback, millionaire.

Number 20, ʊə, is difficult to find a satisfactory English keyword for. Some people use it in *tour* tʊə; but others pronounce this word like *tore*, tɔ or tɒə. Some use it in some or all of *sure, poor, moor, cure, during* (ʃʊə, pʊə, mʊə, kjʊə, djʊərɪŋ); but others pronounce these as homophones of *shore, pore, more,* or rhymes of *four, boring,* with ɔ or ɒə. Then again, many people have ʊə in words such as *fluent* flʊənt, *steward* stjʊəd; rather more frequent, though, are the pronunciations **fluənt, stjuəd**.

In fact *sure, shore,* and *Shaw* may all be homonyms (all being pronounced ʃɔ); but they may equally well all be distinct (being ʃʊə, ʃɒə, ʃɔ respectively). Likewise *moor, more, maw.*

Test these out among the class. What about *poor, pour, pore, paw*—are any of them homonyms? All of them?
Investigate and transcribe your own and other people's pronunciation of the following words—
jury, curious, manure, Europe, brewer, lure, bureau, secure, influence, valuer.
Note that most of these have **j** before the possible ʊə.
Transcribe from dictation—

ɪt meɪ wɜk aʊt.
wɒts ðə deɪt?
du ʃʌt ðə dɔ!
hæv ju gɒt ðə ki ðɛə?
ðə pəʊsts leɪt: ɪts ɪnfjʊərɪeɪtɪŋ!
lɛts tʊə ðə taʊn.

6 Transcribing Connected Speech

EAR-TRAINING
Transcribe from dictation—
kwɪk mɑtʃ. lɛft, raɪt.
deɪndʒə, rəʊd wɜks əhɛd.

English is a language in which one distinguishes STRESSED and UNSTRESSED syllables. Stressed syllables are symbolized by the mark ' placed before the syllable concerned; unstressed syllables are left unmarked. Thus **'ɪnsaɪt** *insight*, **ɪn'saɪt** *incite*.

Say *insight* and *incite* over several times to grasp the idea of stressed and unstressed syllables.

All words when said in isolation, and most words when in a connected passage, have at least one stressed syllable. Study the following examples—

'saɪdə	*cider*
ə'laʊ	*allow*
pə'teɪtəʊ	*potato*
'mɛʒərɪŋ	*measuring*
'kjumjʊlətɪv	*cumulative*

Decide which is the stressed syllable in each of the following words— *collide, bacon, calendar, judgment, another, average, enjoy, bigger, happily, particularly*.

Here is a connected text in transcription, with the stresses marked—

aɪl 'gəʊ ən ɪŋ'kwaɪə wɛðə 'ðɪs ɪz ðə 'weɪ tə ðɪ 'ɛmpaɪə 'θɪətə.

I'll go and inquire whether this is the way to the Empire Theatre.

Say the sentence over, banging out the stress on a desk or chair.

Stress results from a combination of several factors, the most important being extra loudness, extra duration, and change in the pitch of the voice. The recurrence of stresse dsyllables at regular intervals gives speech its rhythmical qualities.

Note the tendency of "function words" (fully grammatical items, such as pronouns, conjunctions, articles, auxiliary verbs, and prepositions) to be unstressed in connected speech. Notice also how many of them are pronounced in connected speech with a vowel (usually ə or ɪ) different from that used when the word is used in isolation. Thus *the* by itself is ði; in connected speech it is usually ðə before consonants and often too ðɪ before vowels. ðə 'bɒɪ, ðə 'gɜl, ðɪ 'ɛnd. (Some people, though, never use the form ðɪ.)

> Find out how you pronounce *the* in each of the following phrases—
> *the chair, the answer, the wheels, the year, the helmet.*

ðə and ðɪ are known as the WEAK FORMS of *the*; ði is the STRONG FORM. Similarly, *at* has a weak form ət (ət 'lʌntʃ *at lunch*) and a strong form æt.

> Discover and transcribe the weak and strong forms of the following words—
>
> *of, was, can, she, them, an, that, for, but, are.*

You are now equipped to transcribe (or write from dictation) a connected English text. Pay particular attention to vowels in unstressed syllables (including weak forms): mostly they are ə or ɪ, whatever the spelling may suggest. Mark all stresses.

EAR-TRAINING

'wɒts ðə taɪm?

'du gɛt ə 'muv ɒn.

aɪm 'gəʊɪŋ 'aʊt fər ə 'mɪnɪt.

'kip 'ɒf ðə 'grɑs.

ə 'stɪtʃ ɪn 'taɪm 'seɪvz 'naɪn.

ðə 'pɛn ɪz 'maɪtɪə ðən ðə 'sɔd.

There are one or two more points about transcription of English to be explained. The symbols l̩ and n̩ denote SYLLABIC CONSONANTS—l and n sounds which are rather longer than usual and have syllable-making function like vowels. Compare 'kɒdlɪŋ *codling* (small cod) with 'kɒdl̩ɪŋ *coddling* (from the verb *coddle*). The word *gluttony* may be 'glʌtəni or 'glʌtn̩ɪ; the latter pronunciation contains no vowel between the t and the n, yet does not rhyme with *chutney* 'tʃʌtnɪ or *Putney* 'pʌtnɪ.

Study the following examples of words with syllabic consonants—

'gɑdn̩	*garden* (childish pronunciation 'gɑdən)
'mɪdl̩	*middle* ("improved Cockney" pronunciation 'mɪdəl)
'bɪtn̩	*bitten*
'bɒtl̩	*bottle*

There is sometimes a choice between syllabic and non-syllabic consonants: *threatening*, for example, can be pronounced either 'θrɛtn̩ɪŋ (three syllables) or 'θrɛtnɪŋ (two syllables).

Transcribe the following—

bundle, hidden, burden, sandals, cotton, cattle, curdled, maddening, bottling, handled.

Write from dictation—

'mɒtl̩ 'padn̩ 'sædn̩d 'mɛdl̩səm mæn'hætn̩ 'gɜdl̩ 'rɒtn̩ 'dwɪndl̩
'pɒtl̩ 'swɪtn̩ 'haɪtn̩ 'pudl̩ 'tʃɒtl̩

In many words pronunciation fluctuates between n̩ and ən, l̩ and l: sɛvn̩ or 'sɛvən *seven*, 'spɛʃl̩ or 'spɛʃəl *special*.

Occasionally other consonants are syllabic, notably m̩ ŋ̍ r̩ as in 'əupm̩ (or 'əupn̩ or 'əupən) *open*, 'steɪk ŋ̍ 'kɪdnɪ (or other possibilities) *steak and kidney*, 'neɪbr̩ɪŋ (or 'neɪbərɪŋ or 'neɪbrɪŋ) *neighbouring*. But do not attach the syllabic mark to any consonant symbols other than m n ŋ l and r.

The symbols ɒə, aə, and ɑə could be dispensed with altogether for some people's speech. For others, though, it is useful to have them available.

Most people do not distinguish *saw* from *sore*, *board* from *bored*, or *cause* from *cores*. They should transcribe the vowel simply as ɔ, thus sɔ bɔd kɔz. Others make a difference, having an opener and/or diphthongal sound in the second word of each pair: we shall transcribe it ɒə and number it 7a. They should write sɔ *saw* but sɒə *sore*, bɔd *board* but bɒəd *bored*, kɔz *cause* but kɒəz *cores*. (Other people again use ɒə where there is an *r* in the spelling, but ɔ where there isn't.)

Investigate which members of the class use ɒə. Can anything be observed about their regional background?

Now consider words such as *fire, tyre, science, pious, liar*. Is the vowel part of these words best analysed as aɪ followed by ə? For some people it is. For others, though, it sounds rather different, being collapsed into a simpler diphthong (or even monophthong) which we shall write as aə.

Decide which transcription is appropriate for yourself and other members of the class—

fire   'faɪə or 'faə
hiring   'haɪərɪŋ or 'haərɪŋ
quiet   'kwaɪət or 'kwaət

Words like *hour, power, towering* are rather similar. They may have aʊ followed by ə; or they may have a reduced diphthong aə; or they may be

23

3

pronounced just like *are*, *par*, *tarring*, in which case of course we simply transcribe ɑ.

> Similarly investigate *power* 'pɑʊə or 'pɑə or 'pɑ, *flowering* 'flɑʊərɪŋ or 'flɑərɪŋ or 'flɑrɪŋ, *sour* 'sɑʊə or 'sɑə or 'sɑ.

In words with the spelling *wh*, most English people pronounce a simple **w**, so that *whine* 'waɪn is a homophone of *wine*, and *which* 'wɪtʃ is pronounced identically with *witch*. Scots, Irish, and many Americans, however, use **hw**, thus 'hwaɪn *whine*, 'hwɪtʃ *which*, and this pronunciation is often considered abstractly correct in England, even though its use is virtually restricted to those who have undergone a certain type of speech training.

> Discuss the question of **w** or **hw** in words such as *when*, *where*, *why*, *whirl*, *whisk*, *whistle*. What about *who*?

Words like *happy*, *valley*, *coffee* end with ɪ in Southern British Standard, thus 'hæpɪ, 'vælɪ, 'kɒfɪ. This is also their pronunciation in many regional accents; but in the local speech of the South of England, and on Merseyside, in the North-east and in Wales, they end in i, thus 'hæpi, 'væli, 'kɒfi. So when making transcriptions of one's own speech one should write ɪ or i according to one's own pronunciation; but when transcribing SBS one should put ɪ.

> Investigate your own and other people's pronunciation of these words: *happy*, *committee*, *donkey*, *city*. Does it make any difference if a vowel sound follows immediately?

Similar considerations apply to words such as *various* 'vɛərɪəs or 'vɛəriəs, *carrying* 'kærɪŋ or 'kæriŋ, *create* krɪ'eɪt or kri'eɪt.

> Discuss the above words and also *maniac*, *prettier*, *react*.

When writing phonetic symbols, be careful to distinguish between æ and ae, a and ɑ, i and ɪ, u and ʊ, ɛ and ɜ and finally z and ʒ.

> Revise any symbols you are unsure of. Write from dictation various alternative pronunciations of *often*.

7 Manner of Articulation

EAR-TRAINING
Transcribe from dictation—
ə 'kwaət 'kɔnə
ɪts 'ɑə 'haʊs
'mɪdl̩ɪŋ tə 'gʊd
ɪts ə 'wɛl 'rɪtn̩ 'bʊk

To identify consonants there are three principal things we have to know. The first two are the state of the glottis (voiced or voiceless) and the place of articulation (bilabial, alveolar, velar, etc.). The third concerns WHAT SORT of articulation is used.

Let us look at alveolar consonants of various kinds.

t and **d** are termed PLOSIVES. They involve the complete blocking of the air-stream.

> Make several **d** sounds and feel the articulation. Note how the tongue tip contacts the alveolar ridge, while the side rims of the tongue complete the closure by contacting the side teeth. The air is thus completely prevented from escaping out of the mouth for as long as the plosive is held.

n is called a NASAL.

> Make several **n** sounds. Feel how the alveolar articulation is identical with that for **d** (and **t**).

The difference between **n** and **d** depends on the SOFT PALATE, the valve that controls the entry of air from the throat (pharynx) into the nose. For **t, d,** and other non-nasal sounds the soft palate is in a raised position to prevent air passing into the nose; but for **n** and other nasal sounds it is in a lowered position to allow air through.

> Thus in **n** air continues to escape (via the nose) even while the tongue blocks any escape through the mouth. Test this by pinching the end of your nose while saying first **n** and then **d**. Note the build-up of pressure during **n** but not during **d**. Why is this?

25

Make a long **m** sound, and see if you can feel the soft palate with your tongue. Curl it back along the roof of the mouth until you feel the soft flesh at the back: this is your soft palate. Then change your **m** into a **b**: you should feel your palate move sharply up and away. Make sure you understand what is happening and why.

A rolled **r** is called a ROLL or TRILL. Rolls are rapid series of closures and openings. So a rolled tongue-tip **r** is a sort of intermittent **d**.

Make a rolled **r** if you can. Compare it with **d**. Contrast **ɑrɑ, ɑdɑ**. If you cannot make a tongue-tip roll, try a bilabial or uvular roll.

Both plosives and rolls involve closure; but for rolls it is rapid and repeated, while for plosives it is longer and single.

Another manner of articulation is LATERAL. In laterals the closure is only partial: air escapes round the sides of a blockage. Our only English lateral is **l**.

Make an **l**-sound as in *leap* **lip**. Try and feel how the sides of the tongue are down, allowing the air out on either side of the blockage formed by the tongue tip on the alveolar ridge. You will perhaps feel this more clearly by making an **l** articulation while breathing in and out voicelessly.

Yet another, very common, manner of articulation involves not a complete closure but merely a narrowing. Sounds of this kind are called FRICATIVES: in English we have alveolar fricatives **s** and **z**.

Make long **s** and **z** sounds. Feel how the air is hindered and made turbulent but not completely blocked as it passes between the tongue and the alveolar ridge. Make an **s** sound with a pulmonic ingressive air-stream (breathing in): feel the cold air along the groove in the tongue beneath the alveolar ridge. Compare this with a pulmonic ingressive voiceless **l**-sound, where the cold air is felt at either side of the mouth only.

These different manners of articulation apply at other places of articulation, too. So **p** and **b** are bilabial plosives, while **m** is a bilabial nasal.

What organs make the closure for bilabial plosives and nasals?

The closure of the articulators in plosives makes the breath pressure increase behind the closure, so that a slight explosion (PLOSION) is heard when the articulators part again.

26

It is also possible to make bilabial fricatives, though they are not used in English. They sound rather like f and v, but are made by narrowing between the two lips instead of between the lips and teeth. (Their symbols are ɸ, voiceless, and β, voiced.)

Try and make ɸ and β. How would you blow out a candle?

f and v themselves are fricatives: LABIO-DENTAL fricatives.
We have already seen that it is possible to make a bilabial roll. It is also possible to make a bilabial lateral.

To do so, get the lips together in the centre but open at either side. Then blow, with or without voicing as desired.

At the velar place of articulation, k and g are plosives, while ŋ is a nasal. Velar fricatives occur in several languages, though not in English. The voiceless velar fricative (symbol x) is like the *ch* in *loch*.

Make voiceless and voiced velar fricatives, x and ɣ.

Sounds such as tʃ and dʒ consist of a plosive followed immediately by a fricative in the same place of articulation. Such sounds are known as AFFRICATES.

Say tʃtʃtʃtʃ and observe the alternation of plosive and fricative segments.
Make the bilabial affricates pɸ and bβ; then the alveolar affricates, ts and dz; then the velar affricates, kx and gɣ. Put them between vowel sounds.
Why are sequences such as ps, kθ, dv not considered affricates?
Make a table with columns labelled BILABIAL, ALVEOLAR, and VELAR, and rows labelled PLOSIVE, NASAL, LATERAL, FRICATIVE, AFFRICATE. Enter as many as possible of the sounds so far dealt with.

EAR-TRAINING
The following are examples of NONSENSE WORDS for dictation. They may be altered or added to by the teacher as desired.
'mʌpt   'sklɔ
'dɛŋz   'tʃəʊp

EXERCISE
Choose a sentence with at least eight different vowel or diphthong sounds in it and put it in phonetic transcription.

8 The Soft Palate

EAR-TRAINING

Transcribe from dictation—

ˡɪˈnɑd   ˈʃtæm

ˈnʌməd   ˈʒɒps

ˈkɒɪgɪŋ   ˈfrʊz

We have already seen (page 25) that the difference between **n** and **d**, or **m** and **b**, lies in whether the soft palate is up (raised) or down (lowered). When raised, it shuts off the nasal cavity from the mouth and pharynx; when lowered it allows air to pass through into the nose.

> We have little or no direct feeling for the soft palate. Repeat the exercise mentioned at the top of page 26.
>
> Say **ama**. Then try to repeat it holding the nostrils. Compare the lack of effect doing the same while saying **aba**. (The symbol **a** denotes a vowel between **æ** and **ɑ**. But in this exercise the precise quality is not important.)
>
> What articulatory difference is there between **ŋ** and **g**?
>
> Say **ama—aba—ana—ada—aŋa—aga** to study the interaction of place of articulation and soft palate position.

The soft palate, then, affects the manner of articulation by causing what would otherwise be a plosive to be a nasal instead.

Consider the word *amber* **æmbə**. At the end of the **æ** the soft palate comes down (and the end of the vowel is nasalized). Then the lips close, and the air-stream is directed through the nose only. This gives **m**. Then the soft palate rises, while the lips remain together: this turns the **m** into a **b**. Then the lips part and the **b** is released; the vowel follows. Note that the **m** and the **b** in this word share the same bilabial closure: as we go from one to the other the only change is the rising of the soft palate.

> Describe the movements of the tongue tip and the soft palate in pronouncing the word *hinder*.
>
> Describe the movements of the back of the tongue and the soft palate in pronouncing the word *anger*.

28

In a word such as *kidney*, where a plosive is followed by its corresponding nasal, an analogous process occurs. In **ˈkɪdnɪ**, after the first ɪ the tongue tip comes up to form a contact with the alveolar ridge, while the sides of the tongue rise to prevent the air escaping laterally: closure for **d** is thus made. Then the soft palate comes down, releasing the blocked air through the nose and turning **d** into an **n**. After the **n** the tongue tip and sides drop again and the soft palate rises as the final ɪ is pronounced.

Describe the articulation of the **bm** sequence in *submerge*.

When someone has a cold he does not, as is often said, talk through his nose: rather, he does the exact opposite, since the nose is blocked, and replaces nasal sounds by the corresponding non-nasal sounds.

Test this out with *good morning* **gʊdˈmɔnɪŋ**: it becomes **gʊdˈbɔdɪg**. Why?

To gain control over the movements of the soft palate, try saying **dndndndn**. Try mispronouncing *Hendon, Camden* German fashion: **ˈhɛndn̩, ˈkæmdn̩** (usual pronunciation **ˈhɛndən, ˈkæmdən**). Between **d** and **n̩** in these sequences the alveolar closure is retained while the soft palate comes down, giving nasal release to the plosive.

Practise non-English sequences **mbɑ, ndɑ, ŋgɑ**. Try these words from the African language Mende (Sierra Leone): **ndovo, ŋgulu, mbawa**.

As **b** is to **m**, so **p** is to voiceless **m̥**. Make it; then alternate **apa, am̥a**. Practise the same thing at other places of articulation: **ata, an̥a; aka, aŋ̊a**.

Say the following English words, releasing the relevant plosives nasally and avoiding the common glottalizing pronunciation—
chutney **ˈtʃʌtnɪ**, *Clapham* **ˈklæpm̩**, *atmosphere* **ˈætməsfɪə**, *topmost* **ˈtɒpməʊst**, *mutton* **ˈmʌtn̩**, *bacon* **ˈbeɪkn̩**.

EAR-TRAINING

Transcribe from dictation—
ˈbmɪmp ˈkɛŋgɒg ˈnɪtn ˈŋukɪ
kəˈlɒsl̩ ˈlɒrɪz ˈkærɪŋ ˈkreɪts əŋ ˈkreɪts əv ˈbɪə ˈbækfaɪərɪŋ əm
ˈbʌmpɪŋ əlɒŋ ˈkrɪkl̩wʊd ˈlem.

In nasalized vowels, such as occur in French, the air-stream passes out both through the nose and through the mouth, simultaneously. Example: *un bon vin blanc* **œ̃ bɔ̃ vɛ̃ blɑ̃**.

(The mark ˜ over a vowel symbol denotes nasalization.)

Try the phrase, not worrying too much about the vowel qualities, but rather concentrating on making sure that the vowels are properly nasalized. Do not insert any **n** or **ŋ** after the vowels.

If you find nasalized vowels difficult to make, proceed as follows. Say a long **m**; keeping everything else the same, open the lips. The result will probably be some kind of nasalized vowel such as **ɛ̃**. Vary the vowel quality to get the vowel desired.

What is the position of the soft palate during a nasalized vowel?

9 The Lips

EAR-TRAINING
Transcribe from dictation—
bməʊˈhʌŋk
ˈkrɪndɪˈdnɔv
pɔˈbumaɪf

There are some sounds, of course, where the lips are the primary articulators: for instance **p**, **b**, and **m**, made by the closure of the two lips, and **f** and **v**, made by an articulation of the lower lip against the upper teeth. But there are also many other sounds where the lips play an important role. These include certain vowels and other sounds which have LIP-ROUNDING.

Positions and movements of the lips are easily observed. The lips are very flexible, and can vary in several ways, including: (1) different degrees of lip-rounding, (2) lip protrusion (usually with rounding), (3) lip-spreading, giving a wide shape. The extent of vertical separation between the lips tends to depend on the jaw opening, though the lips can also move independently in this dimension.

Among English sounds usually given some degree of lip-rounding are the vowels **ɒ**, **ɔ**, **ʊ**, and **u**, the diphthongs **əʊ**, **aʊ** and the semi-vowel **w**; often also the consonants **r**, **ʃ**, **ʒ**, **tʃ**, and **dʒ**.

> Try these sounds, observing your neighbour or using a small mirror to investigate lip positions. As keywords use those shown on the Table, page 17.

A word such as *moon* ˈmun, for example, usually has some lip-rounding, but not necessarily very much.

> · See if you can say *moon* with (*a*) close lip-rounding and (*b*) no lip-rounding. Do the same for *good* ˈgʊd and *law* ˈlɔ. Are these three vowels the same as far as lip-rounding is concerned?

Comparing words such as *cot* ˈkɒt and *caught* ˈkɔt, we see that most English people use considerably more lip action for ɔ than for ɒ. (Scots, on the other hand, don't usually distinguish these two words, using the same vowel in both and making them homonyms.)

31

Most people make the diphthong əʊ with lip movement as well as tongue movement.

> Try the word *toe* 'təʊ and observe possible lip-rounding at the end of the diphthong. Try (*a*) increasing and (*b*) decreasing the amount of lip-rounding you use: does this affect the sound? If so, in what way?
>
> For practice in control over the lips, recite some passage (such as *Jack and Jill went up the hill* . . .) with lip-rounding throughout, and then with none at all—smile broadly as you say it! Can one compensate in some other articulatory way for absence of lip action?

The w sound, on the other hand, seems to need definite lip action. Indeed, the lip-rounding associated with w often extends over other consonants which immediately precede it.

> Say *win* 'wɪn, *twin* 'twɪn, *quin* 'kwɪn, *swim* 'swɪm. Do the t, k, and s have any lip-rounding in these sequences?

Such lip-rounding occurring at the same time as some other more important articulation is known as LABIALIZATION. Thus t does not usually have any lip action; in the word *twin* 'twɪn, though, it is labialized, that is, it has lip-rounding. Labialization is one kind of SECONDARY ARTICULATION. (All labels for secondary articulations end in -ization: others are palatalization, velarization, etc. In each case the secondary articulation accompanies some other, more important, PRIMARY ARTICULATION.)

As mentioned above, many people have considerable lip action for the r in *red* 'rɛd. Some people, indeed, have little or no tongue articulation, though such pronunciation is often considered defective. Note how initial r is often spelled *wr* (e.g. *write, wrong, wrap*), which suggests that this lip-rounding has a certain historical justification.

> Say *red* and other words beginning with r, using varying degrees of lip rounding and protrusion. Try it with a weak labiodental sound (ʋ, discussed in Chapter 22 below) instead of the usual English r. Then do the same with a word where the r occurs in the middle rather than at the beginning, such as *carry* 'kærɪ or *story* 'stɔrɪ. Then say all these words with any other kinds of r-sound you are familiar with.

In one or two local accents the vowel ɜ has lip-rounding—in New Zealand, for example.

> Say *bird* 'bɜd with and without lip-rounding for the ɜ.

EAR-TRAINING

Transcribe from dictation—

ɑə 'faɪn̩l 'mɑtʃ 'daʊn ðe 'mɪdl̩ əv ðə 'haɪstrit 'mʌst əv bɪn əz ɪm'pɒsəbl̩ ə 'spɛktəkl̩ əz 'mɑləʊ əd 'sin fə 'mɛnɪ ə 'lɒŋ 'deɪ.

ði 'ɔdər əv ðə prə'sɛʃn̩ wəz əz 'fɒləʊz:

'mɒmpmə'rɛnsɪ 'kærɪŋ ə 'stɪk.

'tu dɪs'rɛpjʊtəbl̩ lʊkɪŋ 'kɜz, 'frɛndz əv 'mɒntmə'rɛnsɪz.

'dʒɔdʒ 'smɔʊkɪŋ ə 'ʃɒt 'paɪp.

'hærɪs 'kærɪŋ ə 'bʌldʒd 'aʊt 'glædstən 'bæg ɪm 'wʌn 'hænd ənd e 'bɒtl̩ əv 'laɪm 'dʒus ɪn ði 'ʌðə.

'grin'grəʊsəz 'bɒɪ əm 'beɪkəz 'bɒɪ wɪð 'bɑskɪts.

'buts frm əʊ'tɛl, kærɪŋ 'hæmpə.

kən'fɛkʃnəz 'bɒɪ wɪð 'bɑskɪt.

'grəʊsəz 'bɒɪ wɪð 'bɑskɪt.

'tʃizmʌŋgəz 'bɒɪ wɪð 'bɑskɪt.

'ɒd 'mæn 'kærɪŋ 'bæg.

'bʊzm̩ kəm'pænjən əv 'ɒd 'mæn wɪð ɪz 'hændz ɪn ɪz 'pɒkɪts, 'smɔʊkɪŋ ə 'ʃɒt 'kleɪ.

'frutərəz 'bɒɪ wɪð 'bɑskɪt.

maɪ'sɛlf, 'kærɪŋ 'θri 'hæts ənd ə 'pɛər əv 'buts.

'sɪks 'smɔl 'bɒɪz ənd 'fɔ 'streɪ 'dɒgz.

'wɛm wi gɒt tə ðə 'lændɪŋ 'steɪdʒ, ðə 'bəʊtmən 'sɛd: 'lɛt mi 'si, sɜ, wəz jɔz ə 'stim 'lɒntʃ ɔr ə 'haʊsbəʊt?

'ɒn ɑər ɪn'fɔmɪŋ hɪm ɪt wəz ə 'dʌbl̩ 'skʌlɪŋ 'skɪf, i 'simd sə'praɪzd.

33

10 Marginal Sounds of English

Revise the following sounds, not part of the ordinary English sound system—

ʔ m̥ n̥ l̩   (Chapter 3)
ɸ β x ɣ   (Chapter 7)

Transcribe from dictation some nonsense words including them, e.g.

'ɑʊm̥   'ɸɔx   'ɣʌl̩   'βɪnɪn̥   'lʊʔxɜɸ

In some kinds of English, e.g. Scots, the sound x is quite common and has a proper linguistic status (in technical language, constitutes a PHONEME of the dialect concerned—see Chapter 20). But most educated speakers of English use x, or attempt to do so, in at least a few words, including some proper names. The composer *Bach*, for example, is commonly called **bɑx**— with an English-type vowel but a German-type final consonant. And everyone has heard the Scots word *loch* with its pronunciation **lɒx**.

Think of other words with x.
Does any member of the class use x in words such as *technical, monarch, patriarch, architect*? Say the following surnames and place-names with x—

MacLachlan	mə'klɒxlən
Auchindachie	ɒ'xɪnəxɪ
Auchtermuchty	'ɒxtə'mʌxtɪ
Bwlch	'bʊlx
Amlwch	'æmlʊx

A similarly marginal sound of English is the nasalized vowel we may write õ, used mainly in words borrowed from French, e.g. *grand prix* **'grõ 'pri**, *salon* **'sælõ**, *clientele* **'kliõ'tɛl**.

See how members of the class pronounce the words just mentioned. Do some put in an n sound after the õ? Does anyone distinguish in English between the two French vowel sounds ɔ̃ (as in *son* **sɔ̃**) and ã (as in *cent* **sã**)?

Investigate the pronunciation of the following words, where some people use ɔ̃ (or something like it) but others do not—

restaurant
baton
entente
pension (in the sense of "boarding-house")

Transcribe all pronunciations you encounter.
What other words can you think of in which ɔ̃ may be used?

SUBSTITUTIONS

It is a useful exercise, particularly for budding speech therapists and speech specialists, to do a form of ear-training in which English words are mispronounced in some respect: the student has to identify the wrong sound which has been used to replace a correct one. So, for example, *see* might be dictated as ɲi instead of si; the student could either write down the phonetic symbol for the wrong sound, noting also what it has replaced, or could answer verbally, thus "the voiceless alveolar fricative has been replaced by a voiceless alveolar nasal."

Examples of Substitution Ear-training Exercises

For s in *see*: x, ʃ, hw, ŋ;
for f in *rough*: ɸ, m̥, x, θ;
for w in *wet*: v, β, ɣ.

Note that most sounds can be simply and quickly identified by using a three-part label referring to their VOICING, PLACE of articulation, and MANNER of articulation. Thus v, as in *river*, is a VOICED LABIO-DENTAL FRICATIVE; t, as in *tip*, is a VOICELESS ALVEOLAR PLOSIVE; m, as in *come*, is a VOICED BILABIAL NASAL.

Work out the appropriate three-part phonetic label for the following sounds—
n as in *thin*
p as in *peck*
ŋ as in *long*
d as in *order*
g as in *baggage*
θ as in *think*

But we have not yet studied all the labels needed to describe the places of articulation used in English. Note the following additions to what was learnt in Chapter 4.

ʃ   as in *ship* is a VOICELESS PALATO-ALVEOLAR FRICATIVE;

ʒ   as in *measure* is a VOICED PALATO-ALVEOLAR FRICATIVE;

tʃ   as in *chip* is a VOICELESS PALATO-ALVEOLAR AFFRICATE;

dʒ   as in *agile* is a VOICED PALATO-ALVEOLAR AFFRICATE;

r   as in *red* is (for most people) a VOICED POST-ALVEOLAR FRICTIONLESS CONTINUANT.

Practise saying these names until you know them off by heart. (The precise articulations involved are described in Chapters 21–2.)

TEST ON CHAPTERS 1–10

It is useful to do this test (or a similar one devised by the teacher) in order to check up on what you have learnt so far.

A. Here are ten words with *s* in their spelling. Decide whether the appropriate phonetic transcription in each case is s or z—

missing, base, phase, choose, goose, position, consent, rags, bits, edges.

B. Tick the phonetic term which correctly describes the sound indicated by *italics* in the spelling in each of the following—

	Example begin	voiceless ( )	voiced (√)		
1	ha*pp*y	voiceless ( )	voiced ( )		
2	bu*s*y	voiceless ( )	voiced ( )		
3	re*m*ove	voiceless ( )	voiced ( )		
4	*ch*oose	voiceless ( )	voiced ( )		
5	re*d*uce	voiceless ( )	voiced ( )		
6	wi*ll*ow	voiceless ( )	voiced ( )		
7	cri*s*is	voiceless ( )	voiced ( )		
8	wo*rr*y	voiceless ( )	voiced ( )		
9	*s*kin	voiceless ( )	voiced ( )		
10	*l*ie	voiceless ( )	voiced ( )		
11	rou*gh*	plosive ( )	fricative ( )		
12	sta*b*	plosive ( )	fricative ( )		
13	*k*iss	plosive ( )	fricative ( )		
14	ba*th*	plosive ( )	fricative ( )		
15	*v*ote	plosive ( )	fricative ( )		
16	ru*bb*er	bilabial ( )	alveolar ( )	velar ( )	
17	ma*k*e	bilabial ( )	alveolar ( )	velar ( )	
18	co*g*	bilabial ( )	alveolar ( )	velar ( )	
19	*s*tew	bilabial ( )	alveolar ( )	velar ( )	
20	*p*rint	bilabial ( )	alveolar ( )	velar ( )	

C. Underline a suitable phonetic transcription for each word in the following connected passage. (Sometimes there is more than one possible correct answer: choose the one that fits the passage best.)

Jim   and Mary decided they would move into a new house being tired
'jɪm   ən   'meɪrɪ dɪ'saɪdɪd ðeɪ   wʊd   'məʊv ɪntʊ ə 'nu 'haʊs bɪŋ   'taɪəd
'djɪm ænd 'mɛrɪ dɪ'saɪdəd θeɪ   wuld   'muv ɪntu æ 'nju 'haʊs biiŋ   'taɪʒd
'dʒɪm en   'mɛərɪ dɪ'saɪdʌd theɪ wʊd   'mʊv ɪntə eɪ 'njʊ 'haʊs bɪŋ   'taəd

of their flat and wanting more space. They needed a garage for Jim's
ɒf ðɛr   'flɑt ən 'wɔntɪŋ 'mɔ 'space. ðeɪ   'nidid ə 'gærɪdʒ fɒə 'jɪms
əv ðɛə   'flat ənd 'wantɪŋ 'mɒə 'speɪs. θeɪ   'nidɪd eɪ 'gæraʒ fɔ 'dʒɪmz
ɒv ðə   'flæt n   'wɒntɪŋ 'mʊə 'spaɪs. theɪ 'nidɛd ʒ gə'rɑʒ fə 'dʒɪms

car, too.
'cɑ, 'tʊ.
'kʌr, 'təʊ.
'kɑ, 'tu.

The following nonsense-words and English dictation material should be taken down from the teacher's dictation.

'dlɛpm   'wɒdnʌʃ   'ɸaɪdɒʔ   tʃɛ'ɣɒɪʒ   ŋæ'xʒl̩

tə 'pleɪ 'dʒæks, ɔ tə 'gɪv ðə 'geɪm ɪts fʊl 'taɪtl̩, 'dʒækstəʊnz, ðə 'tʃɪldrən 'nidɪd 'faɪv 'smɔl 'raʊnd 'pɛbl̩z. 'ðiz ðeɪ 'tɒs, əŋ 'kætʃ əm 'pɪk 'ʌp ɪn 'vɛərɪəs 'weɪz. bət ðeɪ 'pleɪd 'dʒæk 'strɔ wɪð 'θɪn 'nærəʊ 'strɪps əv 'wʊd wɪtʃ ðeɪ 'θru ɪntʊ ə 'dʒʌmbl̩d 'hip ən 'ðɛn 'traɪd tə rɪ'muv ðəm, 'wʌn ət ə 'taɪm, wɪð'aʊt 'tʌtʃɪŋ 'ɛnɪ əv ði 'ʌðəz.

The English passage may also be used for practice in reading aloud from a phonetic text.

Transcribe this passage—

At a meeting of the Committee of Management of the Royal National Lifeboat Institution for the preservation of life from ship-wreck held at their offices, London, on the eleventh day of March 1937 the following minute was ordered to be recorded on the books of the Institution:

That the Institution gratefully recognizes the services of the St Mary's Life-boat Station, established in 1837 in the cause of life-saving from ship-wreck and on the occasion of the centenary of the station desires to record appreciation of the voluntary work of the officers and committee and the devotion and courage of the life-boatmen of St Mary's who have never failed to maintain the high traditions of the life-boat service.

Total number of lives saved by the St Mary's life-boat by September 5th 1969: 579.

11 Voicing

The test you have just done may have revealed some weaknesses in the detection of voicing. If so, revise what was studied in Chapter 3. Remember that we can observe voicing directly in two ways—

(*a*) by placing the hand on the throat and feeling the vibrations present in voiced sounds;

(*b*) by completely covering the ears and experiencing the buzz of voicing heard in the head during voiced sounds.

> Carry out these procedures for any of the sounds you got wrong in Question *B*. 1–10. Remember that for the procedures to work you MUST say the word out aloud: whispering it won't do.

It's now time to back up the observations we have made by some theory. Look at the following chart of voiced and voiceless sounds in English.

I. *Always voiceless*	p	t	k	tʃ	
	f	θ	s	ʃ	h
II. *Usually voiced*	b	d	g	dʒ	
	v	ð	z	ʒ	all referred to loosely
III. *Usually voiced*	m	n	ŋ		as "voiced sounds."
	w	j	r	l	
IV. *Always voiced*	vowels and diphthongs				

(There are occasional exceptions to these generalizations. Be on the look-out for them and prefer the results of observations to the predictions of theory.)

GROUP I

Test out the sounds in Group I.

Think out two words for each of the sounds in the group, and check whether the sounds are indeed voiceless.

Some people voice **t** when it comes between vowels (when it is INTER-VOCALIC).

Say *butter* and *water* in your ordinary pronunciation. Is the **t** voiced? Then say the same word(s) imitating an American accent, with a voiced **t**.

(If your ordinary **t** in these words is voiced, try to say them instead with a voiceless **t**. What sort of accent does that remind you of?)

Then say the words several times, alternating between a voiceless **t** and a voiced one.

Is a voiced **t** the same as a **d**?

Some people voice **h** intervocalically, too.

Decide whether your **h** is voiceless or voiced in the words *behind, ahead, rehearse*.

GROUP II

Group II, marked "usually voiced," are in fact always voiced between vowels. But they can be voiceless at the beginning and end of words.

Check on voicing of Group II sounds in intervocalic position, using the words *abbey, order, again, lodging, cover, either, fuzzy, pleasure*. (It might be helpful to transcribe them first, so as to be sure what sounds are being investigated.)

A word such as **bɜd** *bird*, said in isolation, will tend to have its **b** and **d** partially or wholly voiceless. In such cases we speak of these consonants being DEVOICED. Note, though, that when the same word is surrounded by voiced sounds, as in the phrase ðə ˈbɜd əˈlaɪts *the bird alights*, the consonants **b** and **d** are fully voiced. When the word is surrounded by voiceless sounds, as in the phrase bət ˈðɪs ˈbɜd ˈsɪŋz ˈswiːtlɪ *but this bird sings sweetly*, we again find devoicing of the initial **b** and the final **d**.

Test these statements: are they true for your pronunciation?

We can summarize by saying that Group II sounds tend to be partially or completely devoiced whenever they are NOT between voiced sounds.

4

Voicing

We can show the voicing pattern of a word or phrase diagrammatically, by drawing a VOICING DIAGRAM like this—

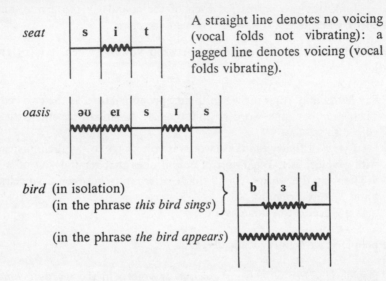

seat

A straight line denotes no voicing (vocal folds not vibrating): a jagged line denotes voicing (vocal folds vibrating).

oasis

bird (in isolation)
(in the phrase *this bird sings*)

(in the phrase *the bird appears*)

Make similar diagrams for the words *face, safe, ticket, assist, faster.* (These should all prove easy.)

Then make voicing diagrams for the word *cab.* (*N.B.* The final sound, **b**, is a Group II sound, and so subject to devoicing.) Show it (i) as said in isolation; (ii) in the phrase *the cab stopped*; (iii) in the phrase *the cab arrived.*

Next make voicing diagrams for the word *gap.* (Here it is the initial consonant, **g**, which is a Group II sound.) Show it as pronounced (i) in isolation; (ii) when a voiceless sound preceded, as in the phrase *this gap*; (iii) when a voiced sound precedes, as in the phrase *the gap.*

When two or more Group II sounds occur consecutively, they behave just like a single Group II sound. So the final consonants **gd** in the word *tagged* **'tægd** are (partly or completely) devoiced before a pause or a voiceless sound—

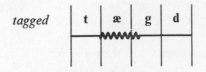

tagged

(The initial **t** here is ASPIRATED (see Chapter 19)—a fact we ignore for the time being.)

40

But they are fully voiced if a voiced sound follows, as in the phrase *tagged it*: **'tægd ɪt**—

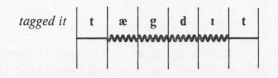

Similarly, the **gb** sequence in *big boy* **'bɪg 'bɒɪ** is voiced throughout (except in the unlikely event of the speaker pausing between the two words).

FORTIS AND LENIS

If the difference between Group I sounds and Group II sounds were merely that Group I were voiceless and Group II voiced, then we should find that this devoicing of Group II sounds would make them indistinguishable from the Group I sounds. Yet **bɜd**, even when said in isolation with devoicing of **b** and **d**, does not sound like **pɜt**. Nor does *this gap* sound like *this cab*. Evidently something more than voicing distinguishes **p** from **b**, **t** from **d**, **f** from **v**, etc.

Group I sounds are more energetically articulated and have stronger breath force than Group II sounds. On this basis we can divide English plosives, affricates and fricatives into the FORTIS (strong) Group I—**p, t, k, tʃ, f, θ, s, ʃ, h**—and the LENIS (weak) Group II—**b, d, g, dʒ, v, ð, z, ʒ**.

> Say *etch* **ɛtʃ** and *edge* **ɛdʒ** in isolation. Notice the difference in force of articulation between the final **tʃ** (fortis) and the final **dʒ** (lenis). Do the same with *rope, robe; calf, calve; place, plays.*

This fortis–lenis difference is reinforced by two further features of the fortis Group I sounds: aspiration (Chapter 19) and shortening of preceding vowels (Chapter 23).

PREPARATION

Transcribe the following passage. (Can you transcribe without referring to the list of symbols and keywords yet?)

> *The weather today will be warm for the time of year and fine on the whole. There will be showers here and there though some places will miss out completely. The good spell should hold over the next two days but there may be fog over low ground in the early mornings. That is the end of the general forecast.*

41

Voicing

EAR-TRAINING

(i) Nonsense words—

'ɣɪtʃɒv   'θuthɑs   'ʔɛəwæɱ   ɑʊ'βɔʒ

(ii) English—

tə 'mʌl 'waɪn. 'kwin v   'tɔrɪəz 'rɛsɪpɪ.

'bɒɪl sɱ 'spaɪs ɪn ə lɪtl̩ 'wɒtə tɪl ðə 'fleɪvə bi 'geɪnd. ðɛn ' æd ən 'ikwəl 'kwɒntətɪ əv 'gʊd 'pɒt 'waɪn, sɱ 'ʃʊgər ən 'nʌtmɛg. 'bɒɪl, ən 'sɜv wɪθ 'krɪsp ʌn'swit d 'bɪskɪts.

12 Voicing (continued); Intonation

EAR-TRAINING

ʃ'ʒɒfθð
'zrɛəgkt
'tʃɪdʒtʃ

GROUP III

Group III, also marked "usually voiced," are fully voiced initially and finally as well as intervocalically.

> Check this statement by saying the words *real, wine, young, male, lemon.* (Note that no English words begin with ŋ or end with w or j. In SBS no words end in r, either, when said in isolation.)

However, most sounds in Group III can occur after other consonants and so form CLUSTERS. In such cases, if the preceding consonant is voiceless, the whole cluster is usually voiceless.

> Say the word 'preɪ *pray* and investigate the voicing of the r. In most people's pronunciation it is devoiced.
> Similarly investigate the l in *play* 'pleɪ, and the w in *twin* 'twɪn and the j in *pure* 'pjʊə.

We can again show this devoicing graphically by drawing a voicing diagram, like this—

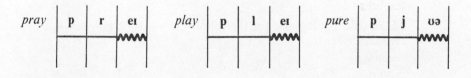

GROUP IV

Sounds in Group IV, i.e. vowels and diphthongs, are in principle always voiced. Occasional exceptions may arise when a vowel is entirely unstressed and between two voiceless sounds.

43

Say the word *success* sək'sɛs. The first vowel is sometimes devoiced: try saying it in that way, and compare it with a pronunciation having a voiced ə.

Do the same with *support* sə'pɔt. If the ə is devoiced, does the word become identical with *sport*?

We are now in a position to make voicing diagrams for any word or phrase. Here is the diagram for the word *common*—

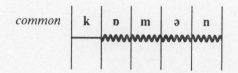

Voicing starts just after the **k** is released. It is switched off again at the end of the word: notice that the final **n** does NOT get devoiced. (Why?)

Here are some more words with their voicing diagrams. Study them carefully and check that they agree with both observation and theory.

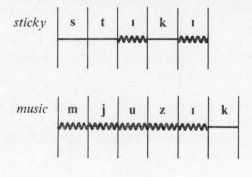

What would these words sound like if ALL the sounds were voiced? If ALL the sounds were voiceless?

Exercise

Make voicing diagrams for the following words or phrases—
crocodile
renewing
grab it
watch them

EAR-TRAINING

These nonsense words aren't easy so be pleased when you identify sounds correctly and don't be discouraged if you get them wrong.

Your teacher will repeat the correct sound and your version of it so that you can hear the difference. Make them yourself and feel as well as hear the difference.

ˈdʒʌtʃʌˈprɪəs   kʊɫˈpʊəkts   ˈxæʔtn̩

INTONATION

By intonation we mean the linguistically significant variation in the pitch of the voice during speech. Changes of pitch, together with features of stress, length, and rhythm, enable us to convey meanings sometimes just as important, though rather different in kind, as those we express through the use of particular words and grammatical patterns. In learning to analyse intonation patterns, ear training is even more important than in other branches of phonetics.

We can start by listening to high and low LEVEL pitches.

>   Listen to the word *two* said with high and low pitches. Then imitate them.

But we rarely use level tones on one-word sentences in English. To see the kind of intonation we might get if *two* was said as a one-word answer in conversation, we have to look at CHANGING pitches.

A falling pitch (usually just called a FALL) is one that goes from a higher pitch to a lower one, thus for example—

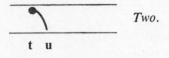

Two.

>   Listen to some falls. Then imitate them. Say the words *now, fine, oh, where*, with falls.

In phonetic notation we can show a fall thus—

ˈtu, ˈnɑʊ, ˈfaɪn, ˈəʊ, ˈwɛə.

A rising pitch (usually just called a RISE), is one that goes from a lower pitch to a higher one, thus for example—

Two?

>   Listen to some rises. Then imitate them. Say the same words *now, fine, oh, where*, this time with rises.

45

In phonetic notation we can show a rise thus: ʹtu, ʹnɑʊ, ʹfaɪn, ʹəʊ, ʹwɛə.

Is it true that statements always have a falling intonation, while questions always have a rise? (How come we can say ˋ*Where?* with a fall? Does ʹ*Fine* have to be a question?)

EAR-TRAINING

Listen to the following words dictated sometimes with a fall, sometimes with a rise. Identify the intonation used.

Right
Ten
Soon
Run

Comment on the speaker's attitude implied by the use of these intonations.

TRANSCRIPTION

Transcribe these lines by Bob Cobbing and indicate some possible falls and rises.

Example: ʹkri ˋzɒk ʹkri ˋzɒk ʹkri ˋzɒk

1. *Cri zok cri zok cri zok*
   Rinkle stammen rinkel stammen
   Tak tak tak tak
   Gros temps gros temps gros
   Temps temps temps tempe
   To two too door
   A door adore
   Toc toc toc toc
   Zzzzz

2. *Bombast bombast*
   Bomb bomb bomb bast
   Bombast
   Emphase
   Em- em- em- phase
   Bombast emphase
   Bombast
   Phebus.

13   Vowel Sounds

EAR-TRAINING

Nonsense words—

ˈpɒp   pɒpəkætəˈpɛtl̩

ˈɒp   əˈpɒsm̩

ˈpɒm   pɒməˈlɒdʒɪkl̩

Analysing vowel sounds is a more difficult task than analysing consonants. This is because a consonant usually has an obstruction at some point in the mouth, and we can easily locate and identify the obstruction. But a vowel sound involves no obstruction in the mouth, although its quality (or TAMBER) does depend on the attitude and position of the tongue. The mouth is really a sort of tube, ending at the lips and with the tongue for a floor; as the tongue changes position it changes the shape of the tube through which the air passes. As the shape of the tube changes, so the resultant vowel tamber alters.

It is usual to classify vowels in terms of three primary variables—

(1) the height of the tongue—how close is it to the roof of the mouth?
(2) the part of the tongue which is highest, i.e. nearest the roof of the mouth;
(3) the position of the lips—rounded or spread?

We can often judge the height of the tongue by investigating the degree of jaw opening. Other things being equal, an open jaw implies an open tongue position, while a narrow jaw opening implies a close tongue position.

Take the words

bead **bid**
bid **bɪd**
bed **bɛd**

What do you observe about the degree of jaw opening when you say these words? Which has most, which has least? What do you conclude about the height of the tongue in the vowels i, ɪ, ɛ?

The following chart shows five English vowels arranged according to the height of the tongue in their formation.

47

i	(*Pete*)	CLOSE tongue position
ɪ	(*pit*)	
ɛ	(*pet*)	
æ	(*pat*)	
ɑ	(*part*)	OPEN tongue position

Notice that the term CLOSE here is an adjective (it rhymes with *gross* and *dose*). Don't confuse it with CLOSED: for a vowel such as **i**, the tongue is not closed but raised CLOSE to the hard palate.

Because of their tongue positions, we call vowels such as **i** and **ɪ** CLOSE vowels, and vowels such as **æ** and **ɑ** OPEN vowels.

> Now try the vowel **u** in *shoe* ʃu. Does it have an OPEN or CLOSE tongue position? What about the sound in *hot*?

Here is a simple diagram of the English (SBS) vowel sounds arranged by tongue position.

i				u	CLOSE
	ɪ		ʊ		
ɛ		з		ɔ	
æ		ʌ			
			ɑ	ɒ	OPEN

(ə can be regarded as having the same tongue position as з from which it differs mainly in length.)

> What can you say about the height of the tongue during the diphthong aɪ? (The tongue starts open and goes to a nearly close position.)
> Now find out about aʊ. (Again open to close.)
> The diphthong ɪə is rather different—how? (The tongue starts rather close and then moves opener to a more central position.)

The second dimension for vowel classification is implicit in the diagram just given. According to the part of the tongue which is highest in the mouth for their formation, we can classify vowels as FRONT, CENTRAL, or BACK.

> Say the vowel **i**, but with an ingressive air-stream (sucking in). The air feels cold at the point where the tongue is closest to the roof of the mouth. Feel how for this vowel sound the tongue is relatively FORWARD in the mouth.

48

Then do the same thing with the vowel ɔ. Notice how the cold part is now at the BACK.

It is convenient to divide the continuous surface of the tongue into several areas—

the TIP   (used in articulating **t**)
the BLADE   (used in articulating **s**)
the FRONT   (part highest in the mouth for **i**)
the CENTRE (part highest in the mouth for **ɜ**)
the BACK   (part highest in the mouth for **u**)

(See diagram of organs of speech, page 13.)

Beware of the term FRONT. Don't confuse it with the BLADE or TIP. Look at your mouth in a mirror while pronouncing **i**. Can you see what the front, blade and tip respectively of your tongue are doing?

We can now add to our simple vowel chart labels showing the PART of the tongue highest in the mouth for the formation of each vowel.

FRONT   CENTRE   BACK

i				u
	ɪ		ʊ	
ɛ		ɜ		ɔ
æ		ʌ		
			ɑ	ɒ

Look again at the organs of speech (page 13). Note that the tongue is the shape of a clenched fist (not long and thin like a dog's tongue). The tip can be pointed, though.

Experiment with the tip of the tongue, pointing and unpointing it. Is it usually pointed while we speak?

The TIP and BLADE of the tongue are easy to see. The FRONT lies under the hard palate when at rest. The BACK lies under the soft palate.

We could draw a cross-section showing the tongue position for any vowel-sound, e.g.

(highest part of the tongue arrowed)

49

But usually we abstract from such diagrams a schematic chart representing the locus of the highest points of the tongue. Marking a point on this chart implies an auditory vowel tamber and a corresponding tongue position

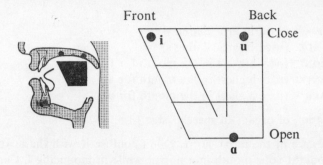

The last main variable we have to consider in vowel classification is the LIPS.

> Say **u**. What do the lips do? (Use a small mirror to find out if you are not sure.)
> It is quite possible to say a sort of **u**-sound without any lip-rounding. Try this. Then say **u** exaggerating the lip-rounding. Is there much effect on the resulting sound?

For most English vowels the lips are unrounded (SPREAD or NEUTRAL). Lip rounding is usually greatest and most consistent with the vowel ɔ.

We are now all set to identify vowels in terms of our three main variables.

	HEIGHT of tongue	PART of tongue highest	Position of LIPS
i	close	front	unrounded
ɒ	open	back	rounded

> (Some people have little or no lip rounding with ɒ.)
> Now try and classify the French vowel **y** (as in *lune* **lyn**, "moon").

y	close	front	rounded

> So **y** differs from English **i** principally by having rounded rather than spread lips. It is difficult for English people to learn since it involves an unfamiliar combination of lips and tongue position. Now analyse the vowel **ɯ**, which occurs in Japanese.

ɯ	close	back	unrounded

To make **ɯ**, do **u** but spread the lips. This, too, is unfamiliar to English ears and mouths.

Analyse the English vowels ɪ and з.

ɪ	fairly close	fairly front	unrounded
з	midway between close and open	central	unrounded

Some vowels vary a good deal in different parts of the country and in different accents. Thus ʌ, as in *love* lʌv, is usually unrounded and fairly open; but it may be fairly back, central, or fairly front (the last being typical of Cockney). In Ireland it is often rounded; in the Midlands and North it is often unrounded but midway between close and open.

> Try out as many varieties of ʌ as you can. Do all the members of the class pronounce *love* in the same way? (A "broader" Midlands or Northern accent has ʊ rather than ʌ, thus lʊv.)

As the tongue moves during the pronunciation of a diphthong, all three variables may change. Thus—

ɒɪ	*from*		
	fairly open	back	rounded
	to		
	fairly close	front	unrounded

EAR-TRAINING

Try the opening of *Richard III*. It's rich in vowel sounds, especially ɑʊ.

> [ˈrɪtʃəd] ˈnɑʊ ɪz ðə ˈwɪntər əv ɑʊə ˈdɪskənˈtɛnt
> meɪd ˈglɔrɪəs ˈsʌmə baɪ ðɪs ˈsʌn əv ˈjɔk,
> ənd ˈɔl ðə ˈklɑʊdz ðət ˈlɑʊəd əpɒn ɑʊə ˈhɑʊs
> ɪn ðə ˈdip ˈbʊzm̩ əv ði ˈəʊʃn̩ ˈbɛrɪd.
> ˈnɑʊ ər ɑə ˈbrɑʊz ˈbɑʊnd wɪð vɪkˈtɔrɪəs ˈriðz,
> ɑʊə ˈbruzɪd ˈɑmz hʌŋ ˈʌp fə ˈmɒnjəmənts,
> ɑə ˈstɜn əˈlærəmz ˈtʃeɪndʒd tə ˈmɛrɪ ˈmitɪŋz,
> ɑə ˈdrɛdfl̩ ˈmatʃɪz tə dɪˈlaɪtfl̩ ˈmɛʒəz.
> ˈgrɪm ˈvɪzɪdʒd ˈwɔ həθ ˈsmuðd hɪz ˈrɪŋkl̩d ˈfrʌnt,
> ənd ˈnɑʊ, ɪnˈstɛd əv ˈmɑʊntɪŋ ˈbɑbɪd ˈstidz,
> tə ˈfraɪt ðə ˈsəʊlz əv ˈfɪəfl̩ ˈædvəsərɪz,
> hi ˈkeɪpəz ˈnɪmblɪ ɪn ə ˈleɪdɪz ˈtʃeɪmbə,
> tə ðə ləˈsɪvɪəs ˈplizɪŋ əv ə ˈlut.

51

Transcription

There is a police message for motorists in the Barnet area of London. A lorry has shed its load at the Apex Corner roundabout on the A1. You are asked to avoid the area as much as possible. South-bound traffic will be diverted for the next two hours. That is the end of the message.

14 Assimilation

EAR-TRAINING

Here are some nonsense words. (Remember that nonsense words are good practice, since they make us concentrate on sounds and forget about meaning.)

tɪʃ ʃɒs pum sɑʊk gɒs deɪg nʌtʃ
bʌv dʒəʊg kɒɪdʒ fɜb məʊf tʃin
haɪp væŋ

Doing dictations in phonetic transcription should by now have made it obvious that many words can have varying pronunciations according to the surroundings they are in—*of*, for example, may sometimes be əv, v, or just ə.

But there are other kinds of variation in connected speech. One of them is called ASSIMILATION.

The word *good* by itself is pronounced gʊd. But in phrases such as *good boy, a good man, good people*, it may become gʊb instead.

Try these phrases out, saying them as 'gʊb 'bɒɪ, ə 'gʊb 'mæn, 'gʊb 'pipl.

In these instances the final **d** of **gʊd** has been replaced by a **b**. This has the effect of giving it the same PLACE of articulation as the following consonant (**p, b,** or **m**—BILABIAL). The articulation of the phrase is thereby simplified, since no tongue-tip movement is now needed at the end of *good*.

Work out just what movements of the organs of speech are needed (i) for the sequence **dm** in the unassimilated pronunciation ə 'gʊd 'mæn, and (ii) for the sequence **bm** in the assimilated version ə 'gʊb 'mæn.

Assimilations of this kind are in fact very common in rapid, colloquial speech, though many people find this difficult to believe. They are fewer in slow or formal speech.

Now let us consider the word *good* when it occurs in a phrase such as *a good cook* or *a good girl*. Here it may be said as gʊg.

53

Try out the unassimilated and assimilated pronunciations. How is the assimilated one simpler to say?

(Notice that in the assimilated 'gʊg 'gɜl the final consonant of *good* is not left out altogether. For the gg sequence, the back of the tongue stays pressed against the soft palate for a longer time than it would for a single velar consonant. Compare ə 'bɪg 'gɜl *a big girl*.)

Assimilations like these may occur whenever a final **d** is followed by a bilabial (**p, b, m**) or velar (**k, g**). They are part of people's ordinary speech behaviour.

What assimilation is possible in the phrases *salad cream* and *broad beans*? Transcribe the unassimilated and assimilated pronunciations.

Can assimilation occur within compound words? (Consider words such as *mudguard, broadcast, headman*.)

In fact the alveolars **t** and **n** are just as subject to possible assimilation as **d** is. (Since it is the alveolar consonants that are affected, this commonest kind of assimilation in English is known as DE-ALVEOLAR assimilation.)

So final **n** may become **m** before a following bilabial, or **ŋ** before a following velar.

Explore what can happen to the word *ten* in phrases such as *ten minutes, ten kings*. (It may become tɛm or tɛŋ respectively.)

The prefix *un-* is often assimilated, thus ʌm'plɛznt, ʌŋ'kaɪnd. But remember that the unassimilated pronunciations occur too.

Construct other examples of assimilation of final **n**, using the words *one* and *in*.

Final **t** may become **p** before a following bilabial, or **k** before a following velar. Thus ðæt 'bɒɪ may become ðæp 'bɒɪ; and ðæt 'gɜl may become ðæk 'gɜl. However many people tend to pronounce the t in such cases as a glottal plosive [ʔ], rather than as an alveolar, and a glottal plosive is not usually assimilated.

EAR-TRAINING

Practise until you can hear the difference between unassimilated and assimilated versions, e.g.

ɒn 'kɔs—ɒŋ 'kɔs
'stænd 'baɪ—'stæmb 'baɪ

Can you distinguish between *that* with a final alveolar [t], bilabial [p], and glottal [ʔ], in the phrase *that boy*? With practice you should not find it too difficult.

Assimilation may occasionally bring about an ambiguity of meaning—
ju 'nid sm 'hɒp mə'njʊə.
ðɛər ə 'raɪp 'pɛər əv 'fulz.
'kʌm ɪn ən 'sɪp baɪ ðə 'faɪə.

But such cases are rare, and the context usually makes things quite clear.

> See if you can think of other examples of assimilation leading to
> ambiguity. (It proves rather difficult to think up plausible examples.
> What do you conclude about some people's assertion that assimila-
> tion is to be avoided because it is lazy and leads to ambiguity?)

In all these cases we saw an alveolar sound replaced by one which is
identical in MANNER of articulation and VOICING but different in PLACE of
articulation. Thus t becomes p or k; d becomes b or g; and n becomes m
or ŋ. It is a characteristic of English that assimilation most typically affects
just place of articulation; in some languages—French, for example—it is
most usually voicing that is affected. English speakers, though, don't assimilate voicing (except some Scots): **'blækbɔd** *blackboard* has no tendency to
become **'blægbɔd**.

There are other alveolar consonants in English which we have not yet
considered. The alveolar fricatives, s and z, are also subject to assimilation,
but only when they are followed by ʃ, ʒ, or j. So **'ðɪs 'ʃɒp** may become **'ðɪʃ
'ʃɒp**, while **'ðiz 'ʃɒps** may become **'ðiʒ 'ʃɒps** and *spaceship* tends to be
'speɪʃʃɪp.

Some people do, and some people don't, assimilate s and z before j. For
those who do, **'sɪks 'jɑdz** *six yards* may become **'sɪkʃ 'jɑdz**.

> Try out the following phrases, all potentially assimilable:
> *yes, you can*
> *these shoes*
> *in all these years*
> What assimilations are possible? Do you think you yourself com-
> monly make them in colloquial speech?

In such cases j may even disappear, and we may speak of the COALESCENCE
of sj into ʃ or of zj into ʒ, thus ɪn **'keɪʃʊ fə'gɛt** *in case you forget*. Another
common kind of coalescent assimilation is the change of tj or dj into the
affricates tʃ or dʒ, for example **'wʊdʒu** *would you*.

PREPARATION: WRITTEN WORK

Show how the final consonants of the words *bad*, *fine*, and *nice* may
be assimilated in connected speech.

Remember that the aim of phonetics is to increase your awareness
of what you do (or may do) when you talk.

READING OR DICTATION PRACTICE

'leɪdɪz ən 'dʒɛntḷmən, ɪn ə 'fju 'mɪnɪts wi ʃḷ bi ə'raɪvɪŋ ək 'glɑzgəʊ.
'pliz 'fɑsṇ jɔ 'sipbɛlts ənd ɪk'stɪŋwɪʃ ʃɔ sɪgə'rɛts. pliz 'steɪ ɪn jɔ 'sɪts
əntɪl ðɪ 'ɛəkrɑft əz 'kʌm tu ə kəm'plit 'stænstɪl. bɪfɔ 'livɪŋ ðɪ 'ɛəkrɑft
'meɪk 'ʃɔ ju hæv jɔ 'hæmbægɪdʒ 'wɪð ju. wi 'həʊp juv ɪn'dʒɒɪd ðə
'flaɪt.

Transcribe this passage—

The Rise and Fall of the River Mersey

"Let us consider Liverpool as a whole" (*Sir James Mountford*).
*The history of this great city is spread around it in the panorama of the
place names of the neighbouring towns and villages. Within the city
boundaries is the great cemetery of the early pioneers, once known as
Boot Hill, now shortened to Bootle. To the north, on the Irish Sea
coast, is the town that kept alive the pig trade with Ireland during the
time of "the troubles," still known to many Liverpudlians by its old
name of Sowport, refined by its inhabitants to Southport. Further north
still is a monument to Liverpool's connection with the slave trade,
once known as New Liverpool, but because of the number of escaped
slaves who made their way there, now known as Blackpool. To the
south lies Runcorn, whose name comes from the corn runners of
eighteenth century corn prohibition.*

*Even over the Mersey, in the peninsula known as Wirral (from the
oft-repeated Lancashire expression "It's luvly today, wirral we go?")
the place names are of great historic interest. Liverpool first had a
mayor in 1352. Up to that date the man who messed everything up
was a lord's bailiff.*

15 Elision

EAR-TRAINING
Nonsense words to help locate difficulties
of aural discrimination—

rʊb θɔk səʊθ rɛɡ fɒɪð θɪʃ mɜ
tɔd ʃɜv tʃus

Once upon a time the words *listen* and *Christmas* were pronounced with a t
after the s. Nowadays there is no pronounced t corresponding to the *t* of the
spelling: the **t** which was formerly pronounced has been ELIDED, historically
speaking.

> Try saying **'lɪstn̩, 'krɪstməs** instead of **'lɪsn̩, 'krɪsməs**. Which pro-
> nunciation is correct? Why? Find out how members of the class
> pronounce *pestle*, then look up its pronunciation in a dictionary.
> Discuss how people pronounce *postman*: which is more usual,
> **'pəʊstmən** or **'pəʊsmən**? Is either of these pronunciations wrong?

But elisions are not just a matter of historical development, as with *listen*
and *Christmas*. Like assimilation, elision affects the pronunciation of words
in running speech.

Consider the phrase *last month*. This can be pronounced as **'lɑst 'mʌnθ**.
But in ordinary colloquial speech it is more usual to elide **t**, giving **'lɑs 'mʌnθ**.

Similarly with the phrase *round the corner*: pronounced carefully it is
'raʊnd ðə 'kɔnə but in faster or less formal speech **'raʊn ðə 'kɔnə**. Here we
say that the **d** has been elided.

> Try out the phrases just given, saying them first without and then
> with elision of the **t** or **d**.
>
> Distinguish carefully between HISTORICAL elision (e.g. *listen*, where
> there is no question of pronouncing the elided consonant today)
> and CONTEXTUAL elision (where the elided and unelided forms are
> both to be heard).

Just like assimilation, elision makes words and sentences easier to say.
Since it does not usually lead to any confusion, it is accordingly very common.

But its nature and incidence differ from language to language, so it is evidently institutionalized and part of our cultural behaviour.

Thus in English assimilation mainly affects the consonants **t** and **d** and the vowel ə. It occurs mainly in the following contexts—

  (i) When **t** follows a fortis consonant and precedes any consonant, e.g. **'nɛks 'wik, ət 'fɜs 'saɪt**.
 (ii) When **d** follows any consonant and precedes any consonant, e.g. **'stæn 'fɑst, 'əʊl 'mæn, 'kaɪnnəs**.
(iii) When ə is between consonants in an unstressed and non-final syllable, e.g. **'mɜdrə, 'næʃn̩, 'trɪfɪk, 'klɒsl̩**. It is particularly common where the strings of ə and **r** occur: both ə and **r** may be elided, e.g. **'lɪtərərɪ** becomes **'lɪtrərɪ** or **'lɪtrɪ**.

Discuss the pronunciation of the words *contemporary*, *believe*, *secretary*, *police*, *probably*, in the light of possible elisions.

Exercise

Take the present-tense and past-tense verb forms *send* and *sent*. Under what conditions do their final consonants tend to be elided? Can this ever cause confusion between present and past? Do the same considerations apply to *fetch* and *fetched*? (Try sentences such as *I'd fetch(ed) them*.)

Notice that the final **d** of *and* can be elided before vowels as well as consonants: **'beɪkən ən 'ɛgz**.

There are many cases where assimilation and elision are both possible, singly or together. Thus *soft cloth* may be **'sɒft 'klɒθ** (full form), **'sɒfk'klɒθ** (**t** assimilated to **k** before **k**), or **'sɒf 'klɒθ** (**t** elided). And *handbag* may be **'hændbæg** (full form), **'hænbæg** (elision), **'hæmbbæg** (assimilation), or **'hæmbæg** (assimilation and elision).

Try out all variants just mentioned. Make sure you can (*a*) distinguish them when dictated, and (*b*) pronounce them at will. Which is your normal pronunciation?

Show how the pronunciation of the phrase *stained glass* may be affected by (*a*) assimilation, (*b*) elision, (*c*) both together.

DICTATION

Either this passage or a similar one with plenty of assimilations and elisions should be written down phonetically from dictation.

'baɪ əm 'baɪ, 'pʊ əm 'pɪglək 'keɪm ə'lɒŋ.

Note the assimilations! If you failed to notice them, practise hearing the difference between the unassimilated and the assimilated forms

—e.g. the teacher should alternate 'baɪ ən 'baɪ with 'baɪ əm 'baɪ until everyone can clearly hear the difference.

'pu wəz 'tɛlɪŋ 'pɪglɪt m ə 'sɪŋɪŋ 'vɒɪs ðət ɪt 'dɪdn̩t 'sim tə 'mætə, ɪf i 'dɪŋk gɛt ɛnɪ 'fætə, 'wɒt i 'dɪd.

Did you get the difference between the alternative pronunciations of *Piglet*? If not, listen carefully while they are compared and contrasted for you.

N.B. 'sɪŋɪŋ, not 'sɪŋgɪŋ or 'sɪŋgɪŋg. (Why not?) The pronunciation with g is of course heard in parts of the Midlands and North of England, and also in New York.

Note the pronunciation of 'dɪdn̩t. If necessary, compare and contrast it with 'dɪdənt. The second time *didn't* occurs, it is assimilated to the following velar.

h is often elided in pronouns when they are unstressed and not initial, thus here i for hi *he*.

How are you getting along with marking the stress?

'lʊk pu, sɛb 'pɪglɪt 'sʌdn̩lɪ, ðəz 'sʌmθɪŋ ɪn 'wʌn əv ðə 'paɪn triz.

Did you get sɛb (assimilated before the p in *Piglet*)? Note the weak forms ðəz (*there is*, *there's*, also ðɛəz, ðər ɪz), ə ðə (*of the*, also əv ðə without elision of the v).

'səʊ ðər 'ɪz, sɛb 'pu, 'lʊkɪŋ 'ʌp 'wʌndrɪŋlɪ, ðəz ən 'ænɪml̩.

Assimilation again in *said*; elision of ə in *wonderingly*.

Note *animal*. Compare the forms 'ænɪməl, 'ænɪmʊl, 'ænɪmʊ often heard in the South-East of England. Discuss final -l̩ and ʊl in *awful*, *careful*, *spoonful*.

Finally, try saying the whole passage with strong forms instead of weak forms throughout ('baɪ ænd 'baɪ, 'pu ænd 'pɪglɪt 'keɪm ə'lɒŋ. 'pu wɒz . . .). Note the resultant effect: like a badly-read script spoken by someone not used to reading aloud. Weak forms, and a modicum at least of elisions and assimilations, give more natural speech.

Preparation

Find a short passage of English. Transcribe it, marking the stress, and hand it in for correction.

PASSAGE FOR READING OR DICTATION

'θæŋk 'gʊdnɪs wi 'sim tu əv 'stɒpt 'θɪŋkɪŋ əv 'mærəʊz 'əʊnlɪ əz 'havɪst 'fɛstəvl̩ ɪg'zɪbɪts əm 'weɪtɪŋ əntɪl ðɛə laɪk 'bærɑʒ bəlunz bɪ'fɔ wi 'ɪt ðəm. ðə 'smɒl 'mærəʊz hæv 'fɑ 'mɔ 'fleɪvə əŋ kəm bi 'kʊkt ɪn ə 'nʌmbər əv 'weɪz, 'fraɪd, 'stʌft, ɔr ɪn ən ʌn'juʒl̩ 'sup, ə 'gʊd 'weɪ əv 'juzɪŋ ʌp ðə 'bɪgə wʌnz.

16   Plosive Theory

EAR-TRAINING

'pliʒ 'ʃʌt ðə `dɔ.
aɪ 'dəʊmp bə`liv ɪt.
Compare—
dəʊmp, dəʊnt, dəʊm, dəʊn.
bɪ'liv, bə'liv.

Quite often in English we get the same consonant twice running, where one word (or grammatically separate part of a word) ends in a consonant and the next word (or part) begins with the same consonant. Thus *penknife* is pronounced 'pɛnnaɪf, with two **n** sounds.

> Say the word *penknife* over. Notice how we usually run the two **n**'s together, making a single long **n** sound.

Similarly, *coolly* is 'kullɪ, with two **l**'s—realized as a single long **l**-sound. Compare *coolie* 'kulɪ, with a single **l**.

(*Note:* the paradox of whether we have one **n** or two in *penknife*, one **l** or two in *coolly*, will be resolved when we deal with phoneme theory, Chapter 20. In these words we have two occurrences of the phoneme concerned, in each case realized phonetically as a single long articulation.)

We get the same thing in a phrase such as *staff fund* 'stɑf 'fʌnd. When the double consonant is a fricative, a nasal, or **l**, it is pronounced just as a single consonant, but longer.

> Try and think up more examples of this and check on their pronunciation. Investigate doubled **m, v, θ, ð, s, z, ʃ**. (Why are doubled **ŋ, h**, and **ʒ** unlikely to occur in English?)
>
> Remember we are talking about doubled sounds, not doubled letters in the spelling—the two *m* letters in *commit*, for example, correspond to only a single **m** sound.

When two identical plosives come together in this way, the results are similar. Thus *book-case* is pronounced 'bʊkkeɪs, where **kk** denotes a voiceless plosive that lasts perceptibly longer than a simple **k**.

> Compare 'bʊkkeɪs with the non-existent word 'bʊkeɪs.

Usually, when two plosives with the same place of articulation come together, they are realized with one long plosive articulation. Occasionally, and in very careful speech, there may be two successive plosive articulations.

> How would you normally say *bad dog*? Are there two **d** sounds here realized as one long plosive, or as two separate ones? Try the phrase both ways, and compare the two possible ways of saying it with **dd**.

To understand more fully what is involved here, we must look in greater detail at the articulation of plosives.

Plosives are sounds in which the air-stream is entirely blocked for a short time: in English, **p**, **b**, **t**, **d**, **k**, **g**. We can distinguish three phases in the articulation of a plosive: the APPROACH (as the articulating organs come together), the HOLD (as they stay together, preventing the air-stream from escaping), and the RELEASE (as they separate and allow the blocked air to escape). Some people distinguish a fourth stage, the PLOSION, when the characteristic noise of the escaping air is heard. We can show this diagrammatically—

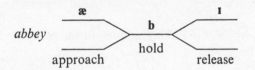

Draw similar diagrams for the plosives in *echo* and *eddy*.

It is useful to distinguish these three phases clearly, since the approach and release phases of plosives may vary considerably according to the phonetic context, whereas the hold phase is relatively free from variation.

In order to make any plosive, it is necessary to have both the nose and mouth blocked off—otherwise the air would continue to escape through the one that was not blocked. Therefore there are always in a sense two closures: the soft palate is raised to prevent the nasal escape, and the lips or tongue articulate in the mouth to prevent oral escape.

In the case of the **b** in *abbey* ˈæbɪ just considered, the soft palate was already raised for the vowel which preceded the **b**. It remained raised for the vowel which followed, and indeed did not move during the articulation of the word.

But now consider the word *amber* ˈæmbə. As we saw in Chapter 8, for the **m** sound in this word, the soft palate is lowered to allow the air out through the nose, and the lips come together to block any air escape through the mouth: as we pass on to the **b** sound, the soft palate rises, stopping any further nasal escape, while the lips merely stay together. They do not need to come

61

together for this **b**, since they already are together. Then, as we pass from **b** to ə, the lips separate in the ordinary way.

> Say over the word *amber*, using a pocket mirror to check that there is only a single lip articulation. Changing from the **m** to the **b** requires no movement of the lips at all. (What does change as we go from **m** to **b**?)

We say that the **b** in *amber* has a NASAL APPROACH, since the approach consists not in the coming together of the primary articulators but in the rising of the soft palate.

The same thing applies to the **d** in *handy*. Here the tongue is the primary articulator, forming a block in the mouth with the tip on the alveolar ridge. For the **n** the soft palate is down; it rises to turn the **n** into **d**.

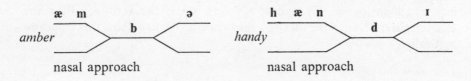

amber   nasal approach   handy   nasal approach

> Show how the same thing applies to the **g** in *anger*. What are the articulations here?

But it is not only the approach that can be nasal, made by a movement of the soft palate only. We can have NASAL RELEASE too.

Consider the **b** in the word *crab-meat* **'kræbmit**. It has an ordinary approach, with the lips coming together to complete the blocking of the passage taken by the air escaping during the æ. (The soft palate is already raised from the beginning of the word.) To turn the **b** into an **m**, all that happens is that the soft palate lowers. This allows the air to escape through the nose and converts the plosive into a nasal. The lips remain firmly closed together: there is only a single closing and a single opening of the lips for the sequence **bm**. (After the lips have separated from the **m**, when the **i** is being pronounced, the soft palate rises again.)

The same applies to the **bm** in *submerge*. Here again the **b** has a nasal release: the release is performed by a movement of the soft palate, not by any movement of the lips.

> Say the words *crab-meat* and *submerge*, observing how there is a single bilabial closure and a single bilabial release for the sequence **bm**. What would the sound be like if the **b** was released separately? Would you ever say them that way?

62

We can have nasal release in just the same way at other places of articulation. In *kidney* **'kɪdnɪ** and *midnight* **'mɪdnaɪt** the **d** has nasal release.

Does saying that a **d** has nasal release mean that air escapes through the nose during its articulation? (No, not during the hold phase— only during the release phase. Where a sound has air escaping through the nose throughout, e.g. **n** or **ã**, we say it has NASAL ESCAPE. Don't confuse the two terms ESCAPE and RELEASE.)

Say whether the plosives in the following words have (*a*) nasal approach, (*b*) nasal release.

end
longer
submit
standing
Rodney
kindness
slumbered
designed

Voiceless plosives can have nasal approach and/or release, of course. Nasal approach for **p, t, k** is quite common: e.g. *lamp* **'læmp**, *rant* **'rænt**, *thank* **'θæŋk**.

Think up some further examples of nasal approach to a voiceless plosive. Describe carefully the articulations involved.

Nasal release of **p, t, k** varies from speaker to speaker. Some people do use it in words or phrases such as *topmost, stop me, greatness, cat-nap, button* **'bʌtn̩**, *steak and kidney* **'steɪk n̩ 'kɪdnɪ**; but many people use glottalization (see Appendix 1) in some or all of these words, which means that the air is blocked by, and released by, the glottis rather than by some organ in the mouth.

Listen to a demonstration of the difference between *button* said with a nasally released **t** and with a fully glottalized **t**. Imitate both pronunciations and make sure you can produce either at will. Do the social connotations of the two pronunciations differ?

INTONATION

We can make a distinction between falls which fall a long way (from high to low) and those which fall a short way (from mid to low).

HIGH FALL   ;   LOW FALL

Two!   *Two.*

We can symbolize falls more precisely thus: high fall, `tu; low fall, ˌtu.

Do ear-training on high and low falls until you can distinguish them with certainty.

We can also distinguish a HIGH RISE (low to high) from a LOW RISE (low to mid)—

HIGH RISE   ;   LOW RISE

Two?   *Two...*

We can symbolize rises more precisely thus: high rise, ʹtu; low rise, ˌtu.

Do ear-training on high and low rises until you can tell them clearly apart.
   Then mix high and low falls. Stick for the time being to one-syllable utterances, e.g.

ʹThem   ˌOut   ˌRight   `All

EAR-TRAINING

(i) Nonsense words

bɪn'nəʊp   yʊ'lɛfθ
'wɛndədnɪp   wim'mux

(ii) English

'lʊk. 'vɪʒn̩ ən ði 'aɪ. 'kɒmprɪ'hɛnsɪv, 'ɪm'mækjʊlətlɪ 'maʊntɪd ɛksə'bɪʃn̩ kʌvrɪŋ 'ɛvrɪ 'æspɛkt əv 'ɒptɪks. ə'nætəmɪ əm fɪzɪ'ɒlədʒɪ əv ði 'aɪ, rɪ'kɔdɪd frm̩ 'ɜlɪst 'grik 'taɪmz. kl̩'ɛkʃn̩ əv 'kweɪnt 'spɛks dɪ'vɛləpt sɪns 'rɒdʒə 'beɪkŋ̩, 'θɜtinθ 'sɛntʃrɪ, 'fɜst 'hɪt ɒn ði aɪ'dɪə. 'hɒrɪfaɪŋlɪ 'bɪg 'kɒntækt 'lɛnzɪz, ɔ'neɪt 'aɪbɑðz, 'vɪʒʊəl 'laɪ dɪtɛktə tə 'kætʃ 'aʊt 'ðəʊz 'feɪnɪŋ 'blaɪnnɪs, 'ɪntrəkət 'daɪəgræmz, 'keɪsɪz əv 'tɔtʃʊəs 'ɪnstrəmənts. 'aɪz ɒn 'stɒks, 'lɪtrəlɪ, fr ɪn'tɜnl̩ ɪg'zæmɪ'neɪʃnz. æn'tik 'maɪkrəskəʊps. 'sɪərɪəs 'kʌvrɪdʒ tə mit 'ɔl 'lɛvl̩z. 'klɪəlɪ ɪks'pleɪnd fə ðə 'leɪmən. ɪ'nɪʃəlɪ ə 'bɪp bə'wɪldrɪŋ. əb'zɔbɪŋ 'wʌnʃ ju 'gɛk 'gəʊɪŋ.

Transcribe this passage—

Human reactions to danger are often archaic instincts, meaning inherited memories, as when a bomb falls through the roof of a building and explodes and the shock survivors absurdly try to scratch a hole through the tiles with their nails—because their remote ancestors would have acted like that in some stage of the human evolution from the three-eyed lizard to hominoid. Nevertheless, the common flying dream is no proof that the dreamer was ever a bird; or indeed, that any of his ancestors were, since palaeontologists deny this link in our evolutionary chain. It seems to be either metaphorical of a wish to fly away from our present circumstances or else—since time is only a convention and memory works both ways; either as reminiscence or as prophetic anticipation—of a future age when human beings will develop wings, as birds once did, and dispense with balloons, planes and rockets.

17 Lateral Approach and Release

Begin with these words, and others, and say them several times for practice on falls and rises.

ˈhɛlp!　ˋheɪ!　ˎlʊk!　ˏhu?

In this next group notice the plosive release.

məkˈtægət　məkˈnɔtn　mæknəˈmɑrə

After the next lines have been dictated, practise them with falls and rises. (If you do this in threes or fours and each do them in your own way and in your own time, you will have the beginnings of a tone poem.)

ˈdɔ əˈdɔd　　ˈdʒækdɔ　　ˈdʒɪl
ˈplɒp　　ˈplɒmp　　ˈplaʊ

As we saw in Chapter 7, the difference between l and d depends essentially on what the SIDES of the tongue do.

Make an l-sound, as in *let*, but keep it on for a long time (a second or so). Then make a d-sound, keeping the hold phase going as long as you can. Feel how in each case the articulation is made by the tongue tip against the alveolar ridge, while the soft palate stays up and the vocal folds vibrate. Ask yourself what the difference is between the two articulations. How does l differ from d?

For the lateral, l, the sides are down, allowing the air to escape LATERALLY without any restriction. But for the plosive, d, they are up, thus preventing the air from escaping laterally; and, since the escape of air is blocked by the tip of the tongue in the middle of the mouth and the side rims of the tongue at the sides of the mouth, whilst the raised soft palate prevents any escape down the nose, the air-stream is entirely blocked and a plosive hold results.

66

Now consider what happens in a word such as *badly* **'bædlɪ**, where **d** is immediately followed by **l**. In such cases the plosive is effected by the lowering of the side rims of the tongue. The dropping of the sides of the tongue is all that is necessary to convert a **d** articulation into an **l** articulation.

– **ædl** – in *badly* **'bædlɪ**.

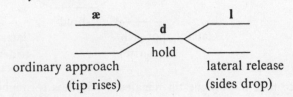

ordinary approach   lateral release

(tip rises)   (sides drop)

Say the word *badly* over a few times, trying to feel the lateral release. Try the further examples *mudlark, oddly, good looks, Dudley*. (Compare the release of the two **d** sounds in the last example.)

It is very common to have a lateral approach, namely when **d** is immediately preceded by **l**, as in *field* **'fɪld**, *seldom* **'sɛldəm**. But here there are the complicating factors—

(i) simultaneously with the rising of the sides of the tongue, an adjustment may occur at the back of the tongue, which has been raised somewhat for the **l** (DARK **l**, see Chapter 19);

(ii) in many accents, notably those of the South-East of England, there is often no actual lateral where SBS has **l**, but just a glide resembling the vowel **ʊ**. If there is no true lateral, there can be no lateral approach.

Say the words *field* and *seldom* in your usual pronunciation and determine whether your **d** has a lateral approach. If not, practise making one.

Henceforth we assume a pronunciation which has lateral approach as SBS.

– **ld** – in *seldom* **sɛldəm**.

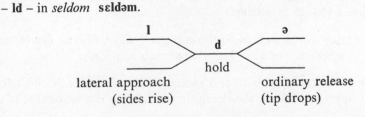

lateral approach   ordinary release

(sides rise)   (tip drops)

67

In a word such as *childlike* 'tʃaɪldlaɪk (said without elision of the **d**!) both the approach and the release of the alveolar plosive are lateral—

– ldl – in *childlike* tʃaɪldlaɪk.

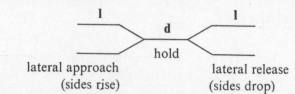

lateral approach   lateral release
(sides rise)   (sides drop)

Notice that the tongue tip remains motionless throughout the whole **ldl** sequence.

In a word such as *middle* 'mɪdl̩ most people have a lateral release to the **d**, the tongue tip remaining still through the **dl** sequence—

– ɪdl – in *middle* 'mɪdl̩.

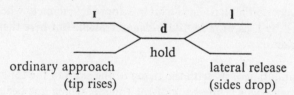

ordinary approach   lateral release
(tip rises)   (sides drop)

Here the **l** is syllabic, but that need not affect the issue. In the South-East of England, though, we again find a tendency to use a vowel-like sound rather than a lateral after the **d**, giving a pronunciation sounding like 'mɪdʊ. Those who have been taught "not to leave their *l*'s out" may then add **l** on to the end of 'mɪdʊ, giving the "careful" pronunciation 'mɪdʊl (or 'mɪdəl) often to be heard from Londoners. In such a case, of course, the **d** does not have a lateral release.

> Say words such as *middle, saddle, curdle, cradles*, and see whether you usually give **d** a lateral release. If not, practise doing so.

Where **t** is preceded or followed by **l**, it too has lateral approach/release— unless it is fully glottalized. (Of course, to go from **l** to **t**, or from **t** to **l**, also requires a change in voicing.)

> Say words such as *bottle, atlas, felt, filter*, finding out in each case whether your **t** has lateral approach or release.

We have now dealt with two special kinds of approach and release. In NASAL approach/release, the change in articulation is a movement of the soft palate; in LATERAL approach/release, the change in articulation is a move-ment of the side rims of the tongue. Since the opposite of nasal is ORAL and the opposite of lateral is MEDIAN, the "ordinary" approach/release, charac-terizing for example the **d** in *eddy*, is properly termed MEDIAN ORAL.

> For each alveolar plosive in the following phrase, state whether the approach and release respectively are median oral, lateral, or nasal—
> *I didn't like getting bundled into the old lorry.*

Notice that, in a long sequence of alveolar plosives, nasals, and laterals such as **ndldn** in *long-handled knife*, the tip of the tongue does not have to move at all. The successive plosive approaches and releases are all nasal or lateral, depending on movements of the sides of the tongue or the soft palate—

	n	d	l	d	n
sides	up	up *	down	* up	up
soft palate	down †	up	up	up	† down

* lateral release and approach
† nasal approach and release

It is a marvellous thing how the human speaker can perform articulatory movements as intricate as these entirely without conscious thought and at very high speeds.

When **l** precedes or follows plosives at some other place of articulation than alveolar, the approach/release is not strictly speaking lateral, though the term is sometimes loosely used in this way. (In *apple* ' **æpl̩** for instance, the bilabial closure of **p** is released by the separation of the lips not laterally but in the median line; but an alveolar lateral articulation is made during the plosive hold, so that the air which escapes on the release does have to escape laterally round the tongue.)

EAR-TRAINING

Transcribe the following passage from dictation—

'lɑs 'taɪm ðə 'bi bi 'si 'sɛnt ə 'kɑ tə k'l̩ɛkt mi, ɪt 'ɔlməʊst 'kæptʃəd ðə 'rɒŋ 'mæn. tə prə'vɛnt ðə 'draɪvə 'luzɪŋ ɪmsɛlf ɪn ə 'tæŋgl əv 'kʌntrɪ 'leɪnz, ðə 'rɒndəvu wəz 'naɪn 'θɜtɪ pi 'ɛm ət ðə 'ləʊkl̩. ɒn ə 'pɪtʃ 'blæk, 'stɔmɪ 'wɪntəz 'naɪt, aɪ bɪ'gæn tə gɛt 'æŋʃəs əz ðə 'klɒk 'krɛpt tɔdz 'tɛn. ðɛn ðə 'lændlɔd 'sʌdn̩lı 'bæŋd ız 'braʊ ən sɛd ðə'wɒz sʌmwʌn 'ɑskıŋ fə mıstə 'raıən ənd i wəz 'sɛnt 'daʊn ðə 'rəʊd tə ðə 'lɒdʒ.

aı 'hʌrıd ə'krɒs tə wɛə mıstə 'raıən, 'mıstıfaıd ənd æprı'hɛnsıv, wəz bıŋ 'bʊlıd aʊt əv 'bɛd. æz aı 'ɛntəd, aı 'hɜd ðə 'draıvə 'seı, 'ıts 'nɒt fə 'ju tə 'nəʊ 'waı. wɛn ðə 'bi bi 'si 'kɔlz fə 'ju, juv dʒʌst 'gɒt tə 'kʌm. ıt 'meı bi 'ðıs ız jɔ 'laıf.

'sʌtʃ ız ðə 'paʊə əv ðəʊz 'drɛdıd ı'nıʃlz 'stıl ın 'rʊərḷ 'ıŋglənd, ıf aı həd ə'pıəd ə 'mınıt 'leıtə, mıstə 'raıən wʊd əv bın 'wıskt 'ɒf tə 'faınd ımsɛlf ət 'mıdnaıt dıs'kʌsıŋ 'gɒd wıð 'mælkəm 'mʌgrıdʒ.

INTONATION

When a fall is followed by a string of unstressed syllables, they are low and level in pitch—

\\'Happiness   \\,Happiness

But when a rise is followed by a string of unstressed syllables, the rise itself is spread out over the whole—

'Happiness?   ,Happiness

This applies equally when the TAIL is quite long, as in the following—
\\'Never, Professor Jenkinson.
'What was it you said you wanted me to do?

Practise hearing the difference between falls and rises with unstressed tails following.

Transcribe this passage—

After living in three countries, Mr. Sachs has noticed that men the world over expect most of their post to be handled by a female member of the family, so why not, he suggests, adopt a form of letter to take care of all usual contingencies? At first sight it's a tempting idea. Picture the damp winter morning, for example, when you simply snatch the pad and mark appropriately the form that reads—

I am sorry my child cannot come to school. He is unfortunately kept at home by measles/his grandmother/your maths test; there is a bus strike/the car has broken down/his mother has broken down; I couldn't find him when I got up this morning.

And another one we could all do in our sleep is—
Dear Mr. Lockjaw, I am sorry my husband will not be able to keep
his dental appointment this week. He is
>*out of town unexpectedly.*
>*the victim of a virus infection.*
>*working for a difficult deadline.*
>*in a blue funk.*

18 Overlapping Plosive Consonants

EAR-TRAINING

Nonsense words—

'dɒkbɛədn   'bmɪɡŋdl
'dlæbd   'tɑlktpm

Transcribe the following passage marking the places where two plosives occur in sequence—

Giveaway newspapers are going great guns. Hardly a week passes without news of another free-of-charge journal being launched. Packed with lucrative advertising, and sometimes devoid of editorial, the "free press" is catching the eye of readers and publishers all over Britain. Post Publications, a stable of nine giveaways, was bought last week by the Manchester Guardian and Evening News group. The price paid is being kept secret. It was founded five years ago by Derek Meakin "with fifty pounds, a kitchen table and a pot of glue."

Consider the sequence **bd** in the phrase *grabbed it* **'ɡræbd ɪt**. It is a sequence of plosives with different places of articulation—the first bilabial and the second alveolar—and in the usual pronunciation of such sequences the two plosive articulations overlap. What happens is that the release of the first plosive articulation does not occur until after the approach phase of the second. For the **bd** in *grabbed it* the sequence of events is (i) the lips come together (approach for **b**); (ii) the lips stay together, while the tongue tip rises to the alveolar ridge (hold for **b**, approach for **d**); (iii) after a moment of double hold, alveolar and bilabial (**b** and **d**), the lips separate while the contact of the tongue tip on the alveolar ridge is maintained (release for **b**,

– **æbdɪ** – in *grabbed it* **ɡræbd ɪt**.

æ   b   d   ɪ

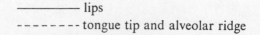

————— lips
- - - - - - - tongue tip and alveolar ridge

hold for **d**); (iv) after a further moment of alveolar hold (**d**) the tongue tip comes away from the alveolar ridge (release for **d**).

The articulation of the sequence **gb** in *Egbert* is similar. The bilabial closure is made before the velar closure is released.

> Work out the detailed sequence of articulatory movements for the **gb** in *Egbert* (as was shown for **bd** above in *grabbed it*).

Similar overlapping usually occurs in English whenever two plosives with different places of articulation occur in sequence. It is usually true of the **kt** in *actor*, the **pt** in *kept*, the **dp** in *midpoint* (unassimilated), the **bt** in *obtain*, the **pd** in *update*, the **kb** in *blackboard*, etc. However these and similar sequences are occasionally pronounced with separate, non-overlapping articulations for the two plosives. This results in a slight **h**-sound or ə-sound (depending on voicing) between the plosives. It is characteristic of most foreign accents of English and also of the careful speech of native speakers of English.

> Listen to the two ways of pronouncing **kt** in *actor*: (i) with overlapping plosive articulations; (ii) with non-overlapping articulations and a brief escape of breath between the **k** and the **t**. Imitate the two forms and learn to produce either at will. Do the same for the **gb** sequence in *big boy*.

The overlapping of plosive articulations means that the release of the first plosive in any such sequence is not audible, since it is masked by the second closure. Hence it is often termed NON-AUDIBLE RELEASE. Another term sometimes encountered, INCOMPLETE PLOSION, is misleading and best avoided.

The "masking" can take two forms. If the second closure is made further forward in the mouth than the first (e.g. **kt**, **dp**, **gb**), then the air freed on the release of the first closure can still not escape, since it is blocked by the second closure. But if the second closure is further back (e.g. **pt**, **dk**, **bg**), then as soon as it is formed it takes the pressure of air from behind the first closure, and again no air under pressure can escape on the release of the first closure.

In fact it is something of a simplification to speak of two closures in some cases—in *actor*, for example, the tongue never really leaves the roof of the mouth during the **kt** sequence, but rolls along it from a velar closure to an alveolar closure.

> Work out what happens during the plosive sequences in the following words or phrases—
>
> *doctor, robbed, stockpot, egg-cup, a locked door, chipped potatoes.*

Things are rather similar when we have a nasal before or after a plosive with a different place of articulation, except that now the movement of the soft palate has to be taken into account as well. The **md** sequence in *Camden*

73

'kæmdən involves the following: (i) the soft palate drops during æ; (ii) the lips close, giving **m**; (iii) the tongue tip contacts the alveolar ridge, as **m** continues; (iv) the lips separate and soft palate rises, giving **d** a kind of nasal approach; (v) after the hold phase of **d**, the tongue tip leaves the alveolar ridge, giving a median oral release for **d**. The **gm** sequence in *dogmas* exemplifies the order of articulatory events when a nasal follows a plosive at a different place of articulation: (i) the back of the tongue rises to contact the velum (median oral approach for **g**); (ii) the lips close, while the velar closure is held; (iii) the soft palate drops and the back of the tongue drops away from it; (iv) after the steady phase of **m**, the lips separate and the vowel follows; (v) during ə, the soft palate rises again.

> Work out the order of articulatory movements during the **bn** sequence in *hobnob*. In what respects does the **pn** sequence in *Stepney* differ?

EAR-TRAINING

ɪt 'wəʊnt 'kætʃ 'faɪə.
ɪt 'wəʊŋk 'kætʃ 'faɪə.
ɪp 'wəʊŋ 'kætʃ 'faɪə.
'dəʊnt bi 'leɪt.
'dəʊmp bɪ 'leɪt.

> Transcribe the following from dictation—

tə bɪ'gɪn ət ðə bɪ'gɪnɪŋ: ɪts 'sprɪŋ, 'mʌnlɪs 'naɪt ɪn ðə 'smɔl 'taʊn, 'stalɪs əm 'baɪbl̩ 'blæk, ðə 'kɒbl̩ 'strɪts 'saɪlənt ən ðə 'hʌntʃt 'kɔtəz ən 'ræbɪts 'wʊd 'lɪmpɪŋ ɪn'vɪzəbl daʊn tə ðə 'sləʊblæk, 'sləʊ, 'blæk, 'krəʊblæk, 'fɪʃɪŋbəʊt 'bɒbɪŋ 'si. 'hʌʃ, ðə 'beɪbɪz ə 'slipɪŋ, ðə 'fʌməz, ðə 'fɪʃəz, ðə 'treɪdzmən əm 'pɛnʃənəz, ðə 'kɒbləz, 'skʌltɪtʃə, 'pəʊstmən əm 'pʌblɪkən, ði 'ʌndəteɪkə ən ðə 'fænsɪ 'wʊmən, 'drʌŋkəd, 'drɛsmeɪkə, 'prɪtʃə, 'plɪsmən, ðə 'wɛbfʊt 'kɒkl̩wɪmɪn ən ðə 'taɪdɪ 'waɪvz.

INTONATION

Falls and rises may be preceded by unstressed or stressed syllables with low pitch.

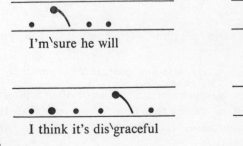

I'm`sure he will

I think it's dis`graceful

I'm‚sure he will

I think it's dis‚graceful

74

Practise recognizing falls and rises, high and low, when preceded and/or followed by unstressed syllables. Remember to listen only to the syllable where the fall or rise occurs (the NUCLEUS) and any following syllables; ignore the pitch of syllables that precede the nucleus.

Say the following phrases with (*a*) a high fall and (*b*) a high rise on the syllable spelt in capitals—

Have you got your BOOKS?
I don't really MIND.
Do stop TALKing about it.
Where would you like to SIT, Veronica?

Transcribe the following passage—

The newly formed National Sheep Association believes in going the whole hog. No nonsense about thinking up recipes for a smart way with half a shoulder: we've been sent a leaflet—its first—for roasting a whole sheep. Roast one, or four, for a teen-age party or charity fete, they suggest. But the economics seem as dicy as most farm figures. Expenditure: up to £7 for the sheep, about £3 for the charcoal, 50p say for the sauce, and £1.25 for the baps to make the Lamburgers. Total £11.75. Income 100 portions per sheep at 12½p a head. Maybe there's a subsidy one can claim.

19 Aspiration; l-Sounds

In words such as *pay* **'peɪ**, *time* **'taɪm**, *carve* **'kɑv**, the release of the plosive is not immediately followed by voicing for the vowel. Between them, there is a period of voiceless escape of breath known as ASPIRATION: we say that the plosives concerned are ASPIRATED.

> Dangle a strip of paper in front of the mouth and pronounce *pay*. The puff of breath constituting aspiration will blow the paper aside on the release of the **p**.

Aspiration is characteristic of English voiceless plosives (**p**, **t**, and **k**), particularly when initial in a stressed syllable. Weaker aspiration, or none, is used with intervocalic **p**, **t**, and **k** ending a stressed syllable, as in *upper* **'ʌpə**, *outer* **'aʊtə**, *looking* **'lʊkɪŋ**. In final position, the amount of aspiration is very variable: *reap* **'rip**, *fought* **'fɔt**, *shock* **'ʃɒk**. After **s**, no aspiration is usual: *span* **'spæn**, *esteem* **ɪ'stim**, *scarf* **'skɑf**.

> Do the strip-of-paper test again, this time with the words *pin* and *spin*. The paper is blown aside with **pɪn**, but not with **spɪn**. Why?

When desired we can symbolize aspiration by a small raised **ʰ**, thus **'pʰɪn**. It is not, however, necessary to show aspiration in ordinary transcription. The voicing diagram for **pɪn** looks like this—

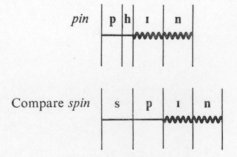

In a sense, the devoicing of **r**, **l**, **w**, **j** after voiceless plosives (Chapter 12) is a form of aspiration: compare *pay* and *play*—

76

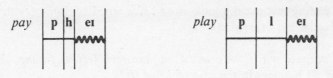

In English it is only voiceless plosives that are aspirated. Languages differ strikingly in whether aspiration occurs in them: in French, other Romance languages, and Dutch, **p**, **t**, and **k** are not aspirated, whereas in other Germanic languages they are.

> Learn to hear the difference between aspirated and unaspirated voiceless plosives. A convenient way of symbolizing them when desired is **pʰ** and **p⁼**, etc., respectively.
>   Try pronouncing phrases such as the following without aspiration:
> *the party of progress*
> *take cover*
> *pass the potatoes, please*
> *carry on, corporal*
> Do any English speakers talk like that?

l-SOUNDS

There is a rather clearly perceptible difference in SBS and most other accents of English between the kind of l used initially, e.g. in **lif, lɛt, lut,** and the kind of l used finally, e.g. in **fil, fʊl, sɛl.** They are both made with the tip of the tongue touching the alveolar ridge, the sides of the tongue being down to allow air to escape laterally (and the soft palate being up to prevent nasal escape). But they differ in QUALITY (or RESONANCE or COLOUR or TAMBER) because of the differing positions of the body of the tongue. The first one, which has a quality similar to the vowel ɛ, is known as CLEAR l; the second, which has a quality similar to the vowel ɔ, is known as DARK l. (More scholarly phonetic terms are NON-VELARIZED and VELARIZED respectively.)

> You can make an l with any kind of vowel quality simultaneously, by trying to pronounce the vowel at the same time as the l, keeping the tip of the tongue firmly in contact with the alveolar ridge. Try this out, pronouncing l-sounds with the qualities of **i, æ, ʌ, ɒ, ɔ, u, ɜ, y,** etc. Then analyse carefully the quality of your l in *less* and *law*, then the quality of your l in *sell* and *all*.

In SBS clear l is used before vowels and **j**; dark l is used before consonants, before **w**, and finally before a pause.

> Decide whether the l-sounds in the following words are clear or dark: *luck, call, milk, shelf, allow, pulse, blame, bilge, silver, silly.*

77

Words ending in l usually have clear l if a word beginning with a vowel follows closely, but otherwise a dark l.

> Compare *sell it!* with *sell!* Compare *feel, feel it, feeling, feel them.* What happens in the case of *I feel ill*?

American English commonly differs from English English by having dark l rather than clear between vowels in words such as *valley, jelly, yellow, pillow*. People from Wales, Ireland, and Tyneside may have clear l in all positions; people from some parts of Scotland may have dark l in all positions.

> Go through all the words with l mentioned in this chapter and try to say them (*a*) all with clear l, and (*b*) all with dark l.
> Does your speech, or that of anyone you know, differ from SBS in the distribution of clear and dark l?

German l is very clear in all positions. So English learners of German, and German learners of English, often have pronunciation problems with l. For example, the German for *milk* is *Milch*. If we use the symbol ł to denote dark l, and the symbol ļ to denote a specially clear l, we can say that English people learning German tend to pronounce **mıłx** instead of **mılç**, whereas German people learning English tend to say **mıļk** instead of **mıłk**.

> Try the pronunciations and mispronunciations just mentioned.

Both clear l and dark ł are usually made with the tongue tip on the alveolar ridge. The difference in the body of the tongue can be shown in a cross-sectional picture of the organs of speech—

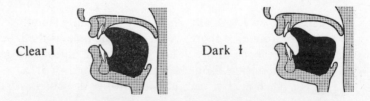

Clear l   Dark ł

As we saw above (Chapter 12), l is sometimes devoiced in English. And it was mentioned in Chapter 4 that it is usually made as a dental, not an alveolar, before θ and ð.

> English dental l is always dark (ł)—why?

78

INTONATION

Another very common tone used in English is a FALL–RISE. The fall and rise can occur on a single syllable—

—or they can be spread over several syllables—

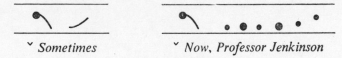

And they can be preceded by other syllables—

But it was ˅ silly of you

Try and analyse the difference in meaning between ˋTwo and ˅Two.

EAR-TRAINING

Transcribe the following verse from dictation. Decide whether the various l-sounds in it are clear or dark.

ðɛəz ə 'blæk 'bɔl 'bɑk
'kʌmɪŋ daʊn ðə 'rɪvə,
'bləʊ, 'bʊlɪz, 'bləʊ.
ðəz ə 'blæk 'bɔl 'bɑk,
'pʊlɪŋ daʊn ðə 'pul,
'bləʊ, maɪ 'bʊlɪ 'bɔɪz, 'bləʊ.

Transcribe the following passage.

Dylan Thomas, say the locals, who claim almost to a man to have been daily drinking companions of the poet, would have enjoyed all the fuss. At any rate, next Wednesday's auction sale of his last home, The Boat House, at Laugharne, has been the biggest talking point in this tiny South Wales township since the party which took place at Brown's Hotel after his funeral. The Boat House which is a damp, unremarkable building built about 140 years ago at the foot of a cliff, has a breathtaking view of Laugharne Estuary with the silence broken

79

only by the seagulls and the Army's guns, which have been shelling off-shore targets a few miles down the coast.

At one time Caitlin wanted Dylan buried in the garden, but instead he rests in St. Martin's churchyard, where a plain wooden cross shrieks for attention among the marble memorials put up to the local dead.

20 Phonemes

Up to now we have been speaking rather loosely in terms of "different kinds of l-sound," "d-sounds with various releases," and so on. But it is now time to look more closely at some of the theoretical concepts and assumptions involved in grouping sounds together in this way—sounds whose articulations sometimes differ quite considerably. We must try and stand back from the material we are dealing with—pronunciations and articulations—and look at them with an unprejudiced eye.

WHY, as speakers of English, do we feel that clear l and dark ł are obviously varieties of "one sound"? Or, again, what is it that the very different t-sounds of *top, stop, pot, eighth, bottle, button, twin*, etc., have in common which leads us to think of them all as being in some sense the "same" sound?

> List the articulatory differences between the t-sounds in the words mentioned.

It is not just that they are articulated in similar ways. After all, there are many other sounds whose articulation is extremely similar, yet we do not think of them as being varieties of the same sound. For instance, the **t** in *twin* has more in common articulatorily with the **d** in *dwell* than it has with the **t** in *button*; so why don't we feel the initial sounds of *twin* and *dwell* to be in some sense the same sound, and different from the sound before the **n** in *button*?

> Analyse the articulations of the sounds just mentioned. Tabulate similarities and differences between the three segments in question. Don't forget the activities of the lips and of the body of the tongue.

The answer seems to be that sounds belonging together in this way are never in direct contrast with one another: we can't distinguish pairs of words just by using one of them rather than another. In most cases the choice of the particular variety of sound used in a given phonetic context depends on that context in a quite direct way. And sounds belonging together do have considerable articulatory similarity.

Putting the last paragraph into proper technical language, we say that particular ALLOPHONES go together into classes known as PHONEMES. Phonemes are CONTRASTIVE with respect to one another. Allophones belonging

81

to a given phoneme are arranged in COMPLEMENTARY DISTRIBUTION (or in some cases FREE VARIATION); they also show PHONETIC SIMILARITY. In the course of this chapter we shall examine these various notions individually.

It is, in fact, the phonemes of English that are represented by the symbols we have been using for transcription of English (page 17)—we have been using a BROAD or PHONEMIC transcription. Other symbols that have been introduced from time to time, e.g. ł, denote not phonemes but either allophones or general-phonetic sound-types considered independently of any language. A transcription using such symbols is termed NARROW.

So l and d, for example, are different phonemes in English. Clear l and dark ł, though, are allophones of a single phoneme: in our phonemic transcription we accordingly write them identically, both as l.

It is usual in linguistic work to enclose phonemic symbols in slant lines, thus /l/, /d/, /fɛl/, but to use square brackets to enclose phonetic symbols denoting allophones or general-phonetic sound-types, thus [ł], [fɛł], [m̩]. (A further commonly accepted convention is that words quoted in ordinary spelling are italicized, or in handwriting underlined, thus *fell*.) We shall follow these conventions from now on.

CONTRASTIVENESS

We can show that two phonemes of a given language or dialect are CONTRASTIVE by listing MINIMAL PAIRS of words distinguished by the contrast (or OPPOSITION) being illustrated. So for English /l/ and /d/ we can list

/lip/ *leap*	—/dip/ *deep*
/lɒt/ *lot*	—/dɒt/ *dot*
/fɛl/ *fell*	—/fɛd/ *fed*
/ˈpʊlɪŋ/ *pulling*—/ˈpʊdɪŋ/ *pudding*	

and so on.

But clear and dark [l, ł] are not contrastive in English—being members of the same phoneme—and there are accordingly no minimal pairs distinguished by the choice between them. We say they are "not in opposition."

List some minimal pairs which are evidence for the contrastiveness of the following English oppositions—
/t/ and /d/
/əʊ/ and /ɔ/
/j/ and /w/
Are there any minimal pairs for aspirated [tʰ] versus unaspirated [t⁼]? If not, why not?

Notice that the contrastiveness of a given pair of sounds in something that varies from language to language—and indeed from dialect to dialect and from accent to accent within a language. This is why transcription symbols given for SBS are not necessarily appropriate for transcribing other accents, whose phoneme systems may be different.

> In Scots accents ʊ and u are not contrastive: *good* and *mood*, for example, rhyme perfectly for the Scots but not for the English. Can you think of a minimal pair to use in order to test whether [ʊ] and [u] are contrastive in a given person's speech?

People learning foreign languages have difficulty when sounds are contrastive in the language being learnt but not in their own mother tongue. This is one reason why English people find it hard to acquire the French opposition /y/ versus /u/, which distinguishes pairs such as *rue* /ry/, meaning "street," versus *roue* /ru/, meaning "wheel." And Germans, for example, find it difficult to get the English opposition /ɛ/ versus /æ/, since they have only one vowel phoneme in the [ɛ—æ] area.

> List some words which become homophonous if the opposition between /ɛ/ and /æ/ is not made.

The same thing applies to people trying to acquire a different accent of their own language. Many Midlanders and Northerners, for instance, start off with no opposition corresponding to that between SBS /ʌ/ and /ʊ/. From the point of view of acquiring an SBS accent, their problem is one of UNDER-DIFFERENTIATION. Not only do they have to learn the different phonetic qualities appropriate for /ʌ/ and /ʊ/, but they also have to learn which of the newly-distinguished phonemes to use in which words—to learn the INCIDENCE of these phonemes in SBS.

> Discuss why some Midlanders and Northerners say, or seem to say, /'kʌʃn̩/ and /'bʌtʃə/ instead of /'kʊʃn̩/ and /'bʊtʃə/.

(Notice that sometimes accents differ in the incidence of certain phonemes without having any difference in their phoneme systems at the point concerned. Contrastive /æ/ and /ɑ/, for example, are found in Northern accents as well as in the South and in SBS; but their incidence differs, in that words like *path*, *grass*, *dance* have /æ/ in the North but /ɑ/ in the South and in SBS. In many Scots accents, on the other hand, there is only one phoneme—we can write it /a/—corresponding to the two found in England.)

COMPLEMENTARY DISTRIBUTION

The kind of /k/ we use before front vowels, in words such as *key* /ki/, is made with the closure rather far forward on the velum—it is almost a palatal sound, [ḵ]. Before back vowels, we make the closure in a retracted, almost uvular, position [ḵ], as in *cool* /kul/.

> Say *key* and *cool* over several times and isolate the initial sounds. Notice the difference between them.

But there is no question of the front [ḵ] and the back [ḵ] being contrastive in English—the difference between them is not one that can potentially distinguish words. (The difference between, say, *keep* and *coop* depends on the vowel contrast between [i] and [u], not on the consonantal contrast between [ḵ] and [ḵ].) In literary Arabic, on the other hand, sounds like [ḵ] and [ḵ] belong to different phonemes, usually transcribed /k/ and /q/ respectively, and words may be distinguished by this consonantal difference alone.

In English, the choice between [ḵ] and [ḵ] is PREDICTABLE from their phonetic environment—when /k/ occurs before a front vowel, it is realized as [ḵ], but when it occurs before a back vowel it is realized as [ḵ]. Before a central vowel, and finally after any vowel, we get a middle quality, [k]. We say that these allophones of /k/ are in COMPLEMENTARY DISTRIBUTION—where one allophone occurs, another can't.

> Check that you understand the notion of complementary distribution. Discuss whether the following pairs of sounds are complementarily distributed in your accent of English—
>
> [ḍ] and [d]
> [n] and [ŋ]
> [θ] and [ð]

The existence of relevant minimal pairs is proof, of course, that two sounds are NOT complementarily distributed.

Where the use of one or another allophone depends upon the phonetic context in which it occurs, we say that the allophones are CONDITIONED by the phonetic context. Thus the allophone [ḵ] is conditioned by a following front vowel, while for the allophone [ḵ] the conditioning factor is a following back vowel. Among the allophones realizing the phoneme /l/, clear [l] is conditioned by the phonetic context "preceding a vowel or /j/", and dark [ł] by the context "preceding a consonant or pause". In such cases we speak of CONDITIONED VARIATION between the allophones concerned.

FREE VARIATION

Sometimes, though, the choice between allophones is free in certain contexts —one or another may occur randomly, and a speaker repeating the same word may use sometimes one, sometimes another without any apparent system. This is called FREE VARIATION and the allophones concerned are termed FREE VARIANTS.

There are occasional instances of free variation in English. Consider the /t/ at the end of a word—*wait* /weɪt/, for example. If the word is repeated several times in isolation (to keep the phonetic context unchanged), most people vary freely between aspirated [tʰ], unaspirated [t⁼], and unreleased [t̚]. (Many use glottalized [ʔt] and even ejective [t'] sometimes, too, but this does not affect the point at issue.) So these /t/ allophones are in free variation in this particular phonetic context. It is just a matter of luck which of them is used on a given occasion.

> Say *Wait*! several times and find out whether you have more than one allophone in free variation for the final /t/.

Note that in other phonetic contexts the variation between [tʰ] and [t⁼] is not free but conditioned—e.g. initially in a stressed syllable we get [tʰ], as in /teɪk/ *take*, but after /s/ we get [t⁼], as in /steɪk/ *stake, steak*.

Some people also have free variation between [ɾ] and [ɹ] for intervocalic /r/ (see Chapter 22).

PHONETIC SIMILARITY

In English, [ŋ] occurs only finally and before consonants, whereas [h] occurs only initially and before vowels. The two sounds are therefore in complementary distribution. So ought we to regard them as allophones of a single phoneme, the variation between them being conditioned by phonetic context?

As native speakers of English we feel intuitively that to call [ŋ] and [h] "the same sound" would be absurd. The theoretical justification for keeping them in separate phonemes is that they do not satisfy the requirement of PHONETIC SIMILARITY. If a given pair of sounds are in complementary distribution or free variation, we do not identify them as members of the same phoneme unless they have the majority of phonetic FEATURES in common. As [ŋ] is voiced, velar, and nasal, while [h] is voiceless, glottal, and fricative, they lack the phonetic similarity which would be necessary for them to belong to the same phoneme. The sounds [l] and [ɫ], on the other hand, share the features voiced, alveolar, lateral, and non-fricative. They are phonetically similar, and we regard them as allophones of the same phoneme. Similarly [tʰ], [t⁼], [t'], and [t̬] all share the features voiceless, fortis, CORONAL (made with tongue tip or blade) and plosive; [ḵ], [k], and [k] are all voiceless, fortis, DORSAL, and plosive.

Forgetting for the moment about the final free variation mentioned above, we can observe that [tʰ] is in complementary distribution not only with [t⁼] but also with [p⁼] and [k⁼]. The justification for classing it phonemically with [t⁼] (as we obviously must) rather than with one of the others is that only [t⁼] has the necessary phonetic similarity with [tʰ].

Go back to the "t-sounds" mentioned in the second paragraph of this chapter. Explain why we regard these articulatorily different sounds as allophones of a single phoneme /t/.

Analyse and discuss the following definition of a phoneme, which is that given by Daniel Jones in his work *The Phoneme: its Nature and Use* (§. 31). "A family of sounds in a given language which are related in character and are used in such a way that no one member ever occurs in a word in the same phonetic context as any other member."

If time permits, study the treatment of phonemic analysis in some of the books mentioned in Appendix 2.

REVISION

1. Check that you understand the significance of enclosing phonetic symbols between (i) diagonals / / and (ii) square brackets [ ]. (Remember that this notation is merely a convention. The same distinction could conceivably be shown by writing one set of symbols in pink and another in yellow.)

2. Check your understanding of the terms in small capitals: ALLOPHONES of a given PHONEME show PHONETIC SIMILARITY. They are arranged in COMPLEMENTARY DISTRIBUTION—that is, are CONDITIONED by their phonetic context—or, in some cases, FREE VARIATION.

TEST

1. Which of the following pairs are CONTRASTIVE in English?

'reɪn—'beɪn   'hʌɾɪ—'hʌɹɪ   'kædɪ—'kæɹɪ   'paʰ—'paˀ

2. Is [ŋ] a member of the English /n/ phoneme? Give reasons for your answer.

3. What is the phonemic status of [ʔ] in English?

4. Describe the various lateral articulations likely to be used in pronouncing the phrase *Lil climbed stealthily*. What reasons are there for classing them together as one phoneme and transcribing them by a single symbol?

TRANSCRIPTION

Frustration is a burst hot-water bottle, or loathing every moment of a holiday you're paying a fortune for. It's using the wrong side of the Sellotape, forgetting what you were going to say, or locking yourself out. Frustration is other people parking in front of your garage, or a stranger reading a riveting letter on the bus and turning over before you get to the bottom of the page.

21 More about Articulation and Intonation

We have already seen that [θ] differs from [s] in its place of articulation: it is dental as against alveolar. But there is another important difference between these two sounds: the shape of the tongue. For [θ] the tongue is relatively FLAT, but for [s] it is GROOVED fore-and-aft along the median line.

> Have a look at the shape of your tongue (or your neighbour's) in the production of first [s] and then [θ]. Experiment with different kinds of tongue shape.

In the case of [s] the air-stream escapes along a groove, but for [θ] it escapes through a slit. So we can call [θ] a VOICELESS DENTAL SLIT FRICATIVE and [s] a VOICELESS ALVEOLAR GROOVE FRICATIVE.

> What is the phonetic symbol for a voiced dental slit fricative? a voiced alveolar groove fricative? Now try and combine the grooved tongue shape characteristic of [s] with the dental place of articulation characteristic of [θ]. This should give a VOICELESS DENTAL GROOVE FRICATIVE, symbol [s̪]. One kind of lisp involves the use of this sound and its voiced counterpart [z̪].

EAR-TRAINING and Sound Production

Recognize and make words such as *six, sack, bus, snake*, with each of the following sounds substituted for [s]: [θ, s̪, x, ç, ŋ, ʃ, ɸ].
Discuss similar substitutions for [z] in words such as *rose, zoo, busy*.

The sound [ʃ], like [s], is a groove fricative; but the groove for [ʃ] is not so narrow as that for [s]. It also extends further back along the surface of the tongue. The place of articulation for [ʃ] is in fact classified as PALATO-ALVEOLAR, since it involves narrowing both between the front of the tongue and the hard palate and also between the blade of the tongue and the alveolar ridge.

> Make [ʃ] and observe its articulation. Alternate [ʃ] with [s] and feel the difference in tongue shape and tongue position between them. Are there any other differences? Is it possible to pronounce either of the two sounds with the jaw lowered? If not, why not?

7

Learn off by heart the following labels: [s] and [z] are ALVEOLAR FRICATIVES; [ʃ] and [ʒ] are PALATO-ALVEOLAR FRICATIVES; [tʃ] and [dʒ] are PALATO-ALVEOLAR AFFRICATES.

DENTAL, ALVEOLAR, RETROFLEX

We have already seen (Chapter 4) that English /t/ /d/ and /n/ are usually realized as alveolar, [t, d, n], although before the dentals /θ/ and /ð/ they are often dental—narrow symbols [t̪, d̪, n̪].

You can think of the diacritic mark underneath as a small tooth to show dentality.

Make [t̪], [d̪], and [n̪] and alternate them with the corresponding alveolars. Learn to recognize them in ear-training—note how English sounds slightly "foreign" if one uses dentals instead of alveolars.

Going in the opposite direction from an alveolar starting-point, we can make RETROFLEX sounds by curling the tip of the tongue backwards and articulating with it in this shape against the alveolar ridge or anterior part of the hard palate. Plosives, nasals, and laterals can be produced in this way: [ʈ, ɖ, ɳ, ɭ].

Alternate retroflexes and alveolars.

EAR-TRAINING or Sound Production Practice

'tæn 'tændɪ'nænæŋ tændɪ'nɑnɪ 'ʈænæŋ tæŋɖmə tæn̪d̪ɪ'ŋɑnɪ tæ'nɑreɪ
tæn̪'d̪itə ʈændɪ'ŋɑnɪ 'tæntɑ'rɑʈə tæn'ɖmə tæŋ'dɪtə
'tænæŋ ʈæ'nɑreɪ tæŋ'kriŋə tæn'rəʊtu tæŋ'ritə ʈæn̪t̪ə'rɑɳɪ tæn'rəʊtu
tæn̪t̪ə'rɑʈɑ tæn̪t̪ə'rɑnɪ ʈæntə'rɑnɪ tæn'ritə tæn'rɪʈə

INTONATION: PLACE OF NUCLEUS

We have studied various intonations—pitch patterns of falls and rises—but we have not yet really seen how they fit into sentences in English or how they are used to convey meanings.

Let us take the sentence *It was a remarkably silly idea.* One way of saying it is with a falling tone on the last word—

ɪt wəz ə rɪ'mɑkəblɪ 'sɪlɪ aɪ 'dɪə

This is quite a natural way of saying it, the way you might reply if someone said to you "What did you think of . . . .?"

But if, on the other hand, you were replying to the question *Was it a sensible idea?*, you would be more likely to say it with a fall on *silly*—

ɪt wəz ə rɪ'mɑkəblɪ 'sɪlɪ aɪ 'dɪə

This seems to put more emphasis on *silly*, reducing the emphasis on *idea*, which is a word simply repeated from the question.

And then again if you were replying to the question *Do you think it was a silly idea?* you might well say

ɪt wəz ə rɪ'mɑkəblɪ 'sɪlɪ aɪ 'dɪə

—putting the fall on to **mɑk**, the stressed syllable of *remarkably*. This puts all the emphasis on *remarkably*, taking emphasis away from the words *silly* and *idea*, which are both now simply repeated from the question. (Note we have kept STRESS constant while altering the intonation.)

Now we can do precisely the same kind of thing with rises, fall-rises, or any other of the tunes we have dealt with so far.

> Try saying the same sentence with a high rise on each in turn of *idea*, *silly*, and *remarkably*.

The word on whose stressed syllable the fall, rise, etc., occurs is thereby thrown into emphatic relief. We say that it (or its stressed syllable) carries the NUCLEUS of the intonation group. The tone which occurs at the nucleus is called NUCLEAR TONE. The place of the nucleus in an intonation group is sometimes called its TONICITY (from the term TONIC, which is a synonym of nucleus).

> Look back at the intonation patterns discussed above. Identify the nucleus in each case. (The nuclear tone was always a fall.)
>
> Take some English sentences such as the following and vary their tonicity in as many ways as possible. Do not worry about the actual tones used, but just about the varying the place of the nucleus.

What did you say his name was?
I flew to Paris last Thursday.
Why don't you relax?
I suppose it's a joke.
Don't rock the boat.

EAR-TRAINING

See if you can identify the place of the nucleus in each intonation group of the following passage of English (to be dictated).

ðə 'brɪtɪʃ 'meɪl, wɪə 'təʊld, ɪz əz 'praʊd əz ə 'pɪnk əbaʊt ɪz 'kləʊðz— ənd əz 'kʌləfl̩ əz wʌn. hiz 'tɜnd ɪz 'wɛl 'tɜnd 'bæk ɒn 'dræbnɪs, ənd ɪz 'ɛvrɪ 'bɪt əz 'fʌsɪ əz ɪz 'waɪf ɔ 'gɜl frɛnd əbaʊt ɪz 'drɛs. 'ʃɜplɪs, 'nɒndɪskrɪpt 'gaɪmənts ə 'nɒt fə 'hɪm.

ɪt 'ɔl 'saʊndz 'vɛrɪ kən'vɪnsɪŋ, bət 'bʌdʒ ən 'ɪntʃ frəm 'kɪŋz 'rəʊd ɔ 'kanəbɪ 'strit ən ðɪ ɪ'luʒn̩ 'sʌfəkeɪts ɪn 'eɪkəz əv 'ɪl 'ʃeɪpən 'klɒθ, 'ræpt əraʊnd 'mɪljənz əv 'mɛn ɪn ðə 'breɪv 'neɪm əv 'kləʊðɪŋ.

ðə 'pɪnk, ɪt 'simz, əz 'fləʊn, ɔr əz 'daɪd ɪz 'fɛðəz 'greɪ tə 'lʊk laɪk ɪts 'neɪbə.

22 English /r/

Nonsense words—

ʧʊədɑn   ɖʌɖ   ʃsɪθs   nwɪɲɒŋ̊

The commonest allophone of English /r/ is a VOICED POST-ALVEOLAR FRIC-
TIONLESS CONTINUANT, narrowly symbolized [ɹ]. It is the sound commonly
used at the beginning of a word such as /rɛd/ *red*, and also in words such as
/brɪŋ/ *bring*, /ə'gri/ *agree*.

> Say /rɛd/ over several times and isolate the first segment, [ɹ]. Try
> and feel where your tongue is for this sound.

This sound [ɹ] is termed "post-alveolar" because it is made with the
tongue tip just behind the alveolar ridge. It is termed a "frictionless continuant" because it is made with the organs of speech in a position similar to
that which would produce a fricative, except that the articulating organs are
not quite close enough together to cause friction. In the case of [ɹ], the air-
stream can escape between the tongue tip and the rear of the alveolar ridge
without any friction. (The term APPROXIMANT is an alternative to "frictionless
continuant.")

[ɹ̩]

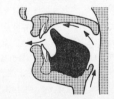

Many people labialize initial /r/, as discussed in Chapter 9.
After initial /p/, /t/, /k/ in a stressed syllable, most people use a VOICELESS
POST-ALVEOLAR FRICATIVE, narrow symbol [ɹ̥]. This occurs in words such as
/preɪz/, /kraʊn/. Moreover, /t/ combines with a following /r/, the two being
realized together as a VOICELESS POST-ALVEOLAR AFFRICATE [tɹ̥]. Examples of
this are found in /traɪ/, /tru/, /'kʌntrɪ/.

Say aloud some words beginning with /pr/ and /kr/; try and isolate the [ɹ] segment. Then say some words beginning with /tr/, and isolate the initial affricate [t̠ɹ], noting that the /t/ and the /r/ have in this case the same place of articulation.

Similarly, /d/ combines with a following /r/ to give a VOICED (or partially voiced—see Chapter 11) POST-ALVEOLAR AFFRICATE, [d̠ɹ], as in /draɪ/, /ə'drɛs/, /'lɔndrɪ/.

Say some words with /dr/, isolating the affricate [d̠ɹ] and feeling how it is articulated.

(The marks underneath the symbols [ɹ] and [ɹ] denote respectively "closer articulation," i.e. fricative, and "opener articulation," i.e. frictionless continuant. The symbol [ɹ] without any diacritic mark can be used when the distinction between fricative and frictionless continuant is not relevant to the point under discussion.)

Between vowels, as in /'kærɪ/, /'sɒrəʊ/, most people use ordinary [ɹ], the voiced post-alveolar frictionless continuant. But others use a VOICED ALVEOLAR TAP, [ɾ]. A tap is like a roll (Chapter 7), except that there is only a single touch of one articulator against the other instead of a whole series of touches. This voiced alveolar tap, [ɾ], is sometimes called "flapped *r*"; there are some speakers of English, e.g. many South Africans, who use it for /r/ in all positions.

Pronounce [ɾ] and alternate it with [ɹ] until you can produce either at will. Do you ever use [ɾ] in your ordinary pronunciation? (Check for its occurrence particularly between vowels and after dental fricatives.) For practice, say the following words with the /r/ realized first as [ɹ] and then as [ɾ] in each case—
right, arrange, ferry, bright, draw.

There are several other sounds which, while not properly members of the SBS /r/ phoneme, are generally thought of as "r-sounds."

The VOICED ALVEOLAR ROLL, [r], was mentioned briefly in Chapter 7. It is popularly supposed to be used in Scottish speech: most Scots, however, use not [r] but a VOICED POST-ALVEOLAR FRICATIVE, [ɹ]. The roll is, however, occasionally used by people in Scotland and elsewhere for special effect, e.g. for declaiming or for extra clarity. And it is used in Welsh and in many foreign languages, e.g. Spanish, Italian, and Russian.

Make a rolled [r] if you can. Try saying various English words with /r/ realized as [r]. Is [r] in some sense the correct way to pronounce /r/? Would you advise a foreign learner of English to pronounce /r/ as [r]?

If you can make a satisfactory [r], devoice it to get a VOICELESS ALVEOLAR ROLL, [r̥]. This is the pronunciation of the Welsh *rh*.

Some English people use a rather different kind of realization for /r/—a VOICED LABIODENTAL FRICTIONLESS CONTINUANT, [ʋ]. (It is also characteristic of the speech of New York City.) It is like [v], except that the contact of the lower lip with the front upper teeth is not firm enough to bring about friction as the outgoing air passes through: one can think of [ʋ] as a very weak [v]. Used for /r/, it is usually considered defective.

> Pronounce [ʋ] on its own and between vowels. Then use it for /r/ in the words *right, arrange, ferry, bright, draw*. Discuss whether this type of pronunciation should be regarded as defective, and if so why. What happens to the opposition between /v/ and /r/? Which well-known public figures use [ʋ]?

Other realizations of /r/ occasionally encountered are the VOICED UVULAR FRICATIVE, [ʁ], and the corresponding frictionless continuant. These are often heard from French and German people speaking English. They are also used by some Northumbrians and North Welsh. The fricative [ʁ] is similar to the voiced velar fricative [ɣ] mentioned above (Chapter 7), but articulated further back, by the extreme back of the tongue against the uvula.

> Pronounce fricative and frictionless [ʁ]. Use them for /r/ in some English words. Does this give the effect of a foreign accent?

The same uvular place of articulation characterizes the VOICED UVULAR ROLL, [ʀ]. This is made by arranging the tongue and uvula so that the uvula vibrates against the extreme back of the tongue in the outflowing air-stream.

> Pronounce [ʀ] if you can. Use a mirror to check what is happening in your mouth. Put [ʀ] in some words. Then devoice [ʀ], giving a VOICELESS UVULAR ROLL, [ʀ̥]. Try whistling while articulating a long [ʀ̥]: this gives a reinforcing effect like a referee's whistle with a pea in it.

One last kind of exotic r-sound is the VOICED RETROFLEX FLAP, [ɽ]. For this sound the tongue starts in a retroflexed position, the tip curled back but not touching anything; the tip is then thrown forward and down, flapping once against the alveolar ridge on the way past and ending up behind the lower teeth. This retroflex flap is used in various languages of India and Pakistan,

93

and sometimes also in the English spoken by those who have [ɽ] in their mother tongue.

Note among the symbols for r-sounds that those which are ordinary letters the right way up denote rolls (r, ʀ), while those which are inverted denote fricatives or frictionless continuants (ɹ, ʁ). Those using the shape of the lower-case letter *r* denote (post-)alveolars (r, ɹ), whereas those using the shape of the capital (or its mirror-image) denote uvulars (ʀ, ʁ).

POTENTIAL /r/ IN ENGLISH

In SBS and most other accents of England and Wales, no word in isolation ends in /r/. So we have, for example, in spite of the spelling, *star* /stɑ/, *four* /fɔ/, *near* /nɪə/. Nor is any /r/ pronounced in these words when they precede a consonant: *starlight, star performance, foursome, four people, nearly, a near thing*; but /r/ may be pronounced if a vowel follows, as in *starring, star attraction, four-ish, four apples, nearest, Near East*. The /r/ used in these latter cases is called LINKING /r/. Alternatively, instead of a linking /r/, speakers sometimes use a glottal stop, [ʔ], or sometimes nothing—but within a single word linking /r/ is nearly universal.

> Say the phrase *four apples* with
> (i) linking /r/
> (ii) linking [ʔ]
> (iii) zero link.
>
> Check that you can recognize these various possibilities with this and other similar phrases.

Linking /r/ is used with words ending in any of the vowels /ɑ, ɔ, ɜ, ə, ɪə, ɛə, ʊə/ and, for those who use it, /ɒə/.

> Think of two examples of phrases with linking /r/ for each of the vowels mentioned.

Historically speaking, linking /r/ is all that is left of a final /r/ that was once pronounced whatever followed—as in present-day Western, Scots, Irish and American accents. But accents like SBS (the NON-RHOTIC accents of English) lost /r/ before consonants and pause two centuries ago: when *start* became /stɑt/ rather than /stɑrt/, *star* became /stɑ/, the older form /stɑr/ being retained only where a vowel followed, i.e. as a variant with linking /r/.

This had an odd consequence. When final /r/ was lost, new rhymes arose: *star—Shah, four—law, tender—Brenda* and so on. Because the first in each pair was subject to linking /r/ when a vowel followed, the second came by analogy to be subject to it, too. A linking /r/ is usual in a phrase like *the star*

94

of Persia: hence /r/ has come to be very common in the phrase *the Shah of Persia* /ðə 'ʃɑr əv 'pɜʃə/. Similar INTRUSIVE /r/'s may be heard in the phrases *law and order, here's Brenda again.* The /r/ is called intrusive in these cases since it was not present historically, is not in general used in rhotic accents, and does not correspond to any *r* in the spelling.

Apart from considerations of spelling, though, linking /r/ and intrusive /r/ are essentially the same phenomenon in present-day SBS. They can be regarded as two forms of POTENTIAL /r/, the difference between them being not strictly speaking a phonetic one. Hence it happens that people who try to eliminate intrusive /r/ from their speech, having been told that it is slovenly or vulgar, can often only do so at the expense of eliminating linking /r/'s too—between words and even sometimes within them.

> Think up two further instances of intrusive /r/ after each of the following: /ə, ɪə, ɑ, ɔ/.
> Discuss whether people are justified in regarding intrusive /r/ as slovenly and vulgar.
> Why is intrusive /r/ (but not linking /r/) virtually non-existent after /ɛə/ and /ʊə/ and completely non-existent after /ɜ/?

INTONATION

One more NUCLEAR tone used in English is the RISE–FALL—

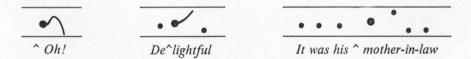

^ *Oh!*   *De^lightful*   *It was his ^ mother-in-law*

> Practise making and recognizing rise-falls. Distinguish them carefully from fall-rises.
> How would you describe the distinctive meaning(s) of the rise-fall?

If you can identify the nucleus of each intonation group and its nuclear tone (high fall, low fall, high rise, low rise, fall-rise, rise-fall), you have mastered the description of the most important features of English intonation.

The pitch features of pre-nuclear syllables are less important. Any unstressed syllables at the beginning of an intonation-group constitute the PRE-HEAD, which may be low or high. Apart from the pre-head, if one is present, any syllables before the nucleus constitute the HEAD. Pitch patterns of heads include high level, downward "stepping," downward "sliding," upward "bouncing," and low level.

TRANSCRIPTION

Use the allophonic symbols discussed in this chapter in transcribing the following passage—

How do you recognize a bargain when you meet one? Right now, take the packet on my kitchen shelf, currently distracting me while I cook. It contains a detergent that recently appeared on the market, and squint-wise across the centre of the packet, is a label proclaiming 3 p off the recommended price. The immediate mental picture is of panic in the factory—Save the customer and reduce the price! Somebody's recommended the wrong one! And the factory leaps into action as it relabels every box. But the law of selling isn't a bit like that. That label is an integral part of the original package; so who recommended that 3 p too much in the first place? See the smart supermarket operator arranging a notice: A free balloon and 3 p plus the original 3 p off. Then running off round the corner to see what can be marked up.

23 More about Vowels

CARDINAL VOWELS

If we consider the vowel sounds that are found in various languages or dialects and try to classify and analyse them, we run up against more difficulties than we do with consonant sounds. Unlike most consonants, vowels do not have an easily perceptible place and manner of articulation. In fact, vowel sounds (or more precisely VOCOIDS, defined as sounds in whose production the air-stream escapes through the mouth over the median line of the tongue with no obstruction in the mouth to its free flow) are most easily recognized and classified by ear—auditorily.

But as we saw in the chapter about phonemes, everybody tends to hear sounds in terms of the phonemic system of his own language. So phonetically naive people tend to hear all vocoids as related to the vowel sounds phonemic in their language. Since different languages have different vowel systems, this leads to chaos if we attempt to classify all vocoids by reference to any given language.

If we were to describe a given sound by saying "it is slightly closer than the /ɛ/ in *get*", this would not be very clear. After all, people vary considerably in how they pronounce English /ɛ/—Australians make it relatively close, Northerners relatively open, and even people using an SBS accent do not all make it precisely the same.

So what we need is a neutral classification system for vocoids—a system independent of any particular language. Such a system was devised by Daniel Jones, and is widely used by phoneticians. It is known as the CARDINAL VOWEL system. The cardinal vowels are particular vocoid qualities selected as reference points for the description of the vowels of different languages and dialects, and have been recorded (e.g. on Linguaphone ENG 252–3). But the best way to learn them is from a teacher who knows them.

Cardinal number 1 is the closest and frontest vocoid that can be made. The raising of the tongue is as far forward as possible and as high as possible consistent with the sound being a vocoid, i.e. with the avoidance of friction. The lips are spread, and the teeth are close together, almost touching. The phonetic symbol is [i]. (Many people find it convenient to distinguish cardinal vowels symbols from those for non-cardinal vowels, e.g. English vowels, by underlining them to show cardinal quality, thus [i]. But this usage, though convenient, does not have the approval of the International Phonetic Association.)

97

Learn to recognize and make Cardinal 1, [i̯]. Compare it with English [i].

The opposite extreme of the vocoid area is represented by Cardinal number 5, [ɑ], which is the openest and backest vocoid that can be made. The back of the tongue is lowered as far as possible and retracted as far as possible consistently with the sound being a vocoid; the lips are not rounded and the jaw is fully open.

Learn to recognize and make Cardinal 5, [ɑ]. Compare it with English [ɑ].

Cardinals number 2, 3, and 4 (symbols [e̱], [ɛ], [a̱]) are front vowels falling between [i̱] and [ɑ̱], chosen in such a way that the intervals between adjacent cardinal vowels form a series of auditorily equal steps.

Learn to recognize and make Cardinals 2, 3, and 4—[e̱, ɛ, a̱]. Compare them with English [ɪ, eɪ, ɛ, ɛə, æ, ʌ].

Cardinals 6, 7, and 8 (symbols [ɔ], [o̱], [u̱]) are back vowels with lip-rounding. They are chosen so as to continue the series of auditorily equidistant steps [i̱—e̱—ɛ—a̱—ɑ̱—ɔ—o̱—u̱]. The lips are OPEN-ROUNDED for [ɔ], close rounded for [o̱], and closer rounded still for [u̱].

Learn to make and recognize Cardinals 6, 7, and 8—[ɔ, o̱, u̱]. Compare them with English [ɒ, ɔ, əʊ, ʊ, u].

The eight PRIMARY cardinal vowels dealt with so far are the basis of the VOWEL CHART diagram often used in phonetics works (Chapter 13). It represents the presumed position of the highest point of the tongue in the mouth: in fact it is a schematization of the LOCUS of the highest point of the tongue (although a point is generally placed on it by auditory rather than articulatory identification).

Vowels

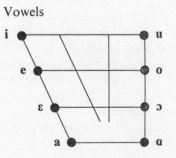

Study the following diagrams showing English (SBS) typical vowel qualities placed on the vowel chart.

Monophthongs

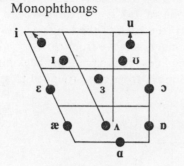

Closing diphthongs   Centring diphthongs

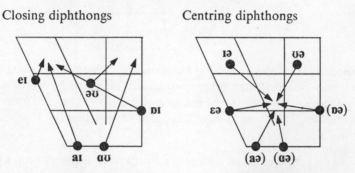

Monophthongs are vocoids during the production of which the tongue and lips stay in the same position, so that the resultant sound does not change; diphthongs are vocoids during the production of which the tongue and/or lips move, so that the resultant sound changes as it proceeds (Chapter 13). Among the English vowels shown on the chart of monophthongs, /i/ and /u/ are often actually rather diphthongal, [ɪi, ʊu], particularly when stressed and final: *sea, two*.

Diphthongs are termed CLOSING if their second element involves a move to a closer tongue position; they are termed CENTRING if their second element involves a move to a central position. All the English diphthongs listed are DIMINUENDO (or FALLING) in that their second element is less prominent than their first. Sometimes the /ɪə/ sequence in *happier* /'hæpɪə/, etc., and the /ʊə/ sequence in *influence* /'ɪnflʊəns/, etc., are analysed as CRESCENDO (or RISING) diphthongs, since their second elements have greater prominence than their first.

ENGLISH SEMIVOWELS

The English PALATAL SEMIVOWEL /j/ as in *yes* /jɛs/, and LABIO-VELAR SEMI-VOWEL /w/, as in *wet* /wɛt/ are usually vocoids, but very short and gliding

99

ones. The commonest allophone of /j/ is a relatively front close unrounded vocoid, [ĭ] or [ɪ̆] (the mark ˘ shows that the sound concerned is non-syllabic). In /jɛs/ the front of tongue glides from a close to a nearly half-open position, [ĭɛ]. Similarly, the commonest allophone of /w/ is a relatively back close rounded vocoid, [ŭ] or [ŏ]. In *what* /wɒt/ the back of the tongue glides from a close to a nearly open position, while the lips move from close-rounded to open-rounded, [ŭɒ]. In /wɛt/ the tongue glides from having the back highest, from close to nearly half-open; the lips move from close-rounded to spread.

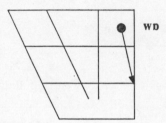

Occasionally, though, /j/ and /w/ have fricative allophones—notably after /p, t, k/, and perhaps after other voiceless consonants. In words such as *pure* /pjʊə/, *queue* /kju/, /j/ is realized as a VOICELESS PALATAL FRICATIVE, [ç]. (And /k/ before /j/ becomes more or less palatal too so that /kj/ is pronounced [kç] or [cç].)

> Say over *pure*, *queue*, and other words with sequences /pj, kj/. Feel the articulation involved for /j/. Try and isolate the [ç] segment. What part of the tongue is it made with?
> Then try *tune* and *Tuesday*. Do you say these with /tʃ/ or with /tj/? If the latter, how is the /j/ realized? Possibly as [ç] (see next chapter).

The sequence /hj/, as in *huge*, may be realized by a single segment [ç], or by a less fricative sequence.

> Isolate the first sound in your pronunciation of *human*.

In words such as *twin* /twɪn/, *quite* /kwaɪt/, the /w/ is realized as a VOICELESS LABIO-VELAR FRICATIVE, [ʍ], articulated by the back of the tongue near the velum and with the lips closely rounded.

> Say these and other words with /tw/, /kw/. Try to isolate the [ʍ] segment.

We have seen that /j/ and /w/ are typically vocoid—like vowels. So the question arises, what is special about them that makes us separate them from vowels and put them in a distinct category called "semi-vowels"?

It is a matter of their place in the STRUCTURE of the syllable. An English syllable has the structural formula

$$C_0^3 \ V \ C_0^4$$

i.e. from zero to three initial consonants, followed by a vowel (monophthong or diphthong), followed by zero to four final consonants.

To avoid complications, let us consider just words of one syllable, with the structure C V, i.e. one consonant plus one vowel. Examples are—

key /ki/
saw /sɔ/
now /naʊ/
bar /bɑ/
foe /fəʊ/
day /deɪ/   etc.

If we take monosyllabic words of this type containing /j/ or /w/, we find that the /j/ or /w/ can only come in the C place, never in the V place—

you /ju/
we /wi/
year /jɜ/ or /jɪə/
war /wɔ/
why /waɪ/

We cannot have words of the type */bj/, */kw/ etc. In other words, semi-vowels BEHAVE AS CONSONANTS, even though articulatorily they are like vowels (vocoid). We say that consonants, including semi-vowels, have MARGINAL syllabic function, whereas vowels have CENTRAL syllabic function (on the basis of CVC syllables).

> Taking syllables of the structure CVC (e.g. *bet* /bɛt/), show how /j/ and /w/ behave as consonants rather than vowels. Do you notice anything about (i) the vowels that occur in (C)VC monosyllables but not in (C)V monosyllables? (ii) the restriction of certain consonants to either initial or final C place?
>
> What place in syllable structure do syllabic consonants—/l̩, n̩/—occupy? How does this compare with their articulatory classification? Is there a case for labelling them SEMI-CONSONANTS?

DURATION OF ENGLISH VOWELS

The English monophthongs can be divided into the SHORT monophthongs, /ɪ, ɛ, æ, ʌ, ɒ, ʊ, ə/, and the LONG monophthongs, /i, ɑ, ɔ, u, ɜ/. Other things being equal, the long vowels have greater duration than the short ones. The diphthongs are comparable in duration to the long monophthongs.

> To check this, compare *bid* with *bead*, *nod* with *gnawed*, etc.

101

But the realization of all vowels varies considerably in duration according to phonetic context. The long vowels and diphthongs are particularly affected by phonetic context. The most important factors are—

(1) A following FORTIS consonant—one of /p t k tʃ f θ s ʃ/.
(2) A following UNSTRESSED syllable, or several such syllables, within the same word or stress group.
(3) Occurrence in an unstressed syllable immediately followed by a strongly stressed one.

Each of these contexts has the effect of SHORTENING the duration of a vowel, though without changing its quality.

> Compare the /i/ in *see*, *need* (fully long), with those in (1) *seat*, (2) *cedar*, (3) *Seattle*. Which of the three shortening contexts has the strongest shortening effect?
>
> Discuss the duration of /ɔ/ allophones in *law*, *lawn*, *talk*, *order*, *austere*.
>
> Think up sets of words to illustrate variations of duration for /u/ and /aɪ/.

EAR-TRAINING
Nonsense words—

ˈjwaθjaz   ˈçɔdiʒ   vɪ ˈvɛde jɔk   ˈhjaçuv

Transcribe the following passage from dictation—

ˈaɪ ˈzɪli ɜˈheɪ
ˈzɔn aˈskɛl
wɪlfrɪ ˈbavæs
ˈbivɛn oˈdet ˈbɔvɪn
ˈbiban ˈtriɡ ˈbuban
ˈtizuk kɛˈlɛvɑjinə ˈtɛzɪk,
stɪˈfok kaˈpruz steˈfak
kɔˈbɛstɑ ˈspoçɛl çaˈbitɔ.

When you have checked the accuracy of your phonetic transcription of the following passage, underline short vowels in red, long vowels in another colour; and double the line for those whose phonetic context gives them a long duration.

ɪn ən ˈaɪdɪəl ˈwɜld, ðɛə wʊd bi ə ˈɡreɪt ˈnʌmbər əv ˈdɪfrənt ˈsɔts əv ˈskul. ˈɔl wʊd bi ˈfri fə ˈɛvrɪbɒdɪ, əm ˈpɛərənts kʊd ˈtʃuz wɒt wəz ˈbɛst fə ðɛə ˈtʃɪldrən wɪðaʊt kənsɪdəˈreɪʃn əv ˈmʌnɪ, ˈdɪstrɪkt, ˈklɑs ɔ ˈɡrɑft. wi wɪl ˈnɑʊ hæv ˈtu ˈmɪnɪts ˈsaɪləns tə ˈkɒntɛmpleɪt ðɪ ʌnˈlaɪklɪ ˈprɒspɛkt.

24 Other Sound-types

In this chapter we shall look briefly at quite a large number of sound-types, some of them rather exotic. You will probably find this concentrated diet quite indigestible if you try to swallow everything at once. To assimilate the material thoroughly, you will need to do a lot of regular practice in—

(1) ear-training—recognizing different sound-types when produced by the teacher or another student;

(2) description—identifying the articulation used to produce a given sound-type;

(3) sound production—making the sounds yourself.

1. PALATAL, VELAR, UVULAR

Raise the back of your tongue to form a [k] closure against the velum. Note where the tip of your tongue is—behind the lower teeth, out of the way. Keep the tip down while feeling forward from the velum until the FRONT of the tongue (NOT the blade or tip) is articulating against the HARD PALATE. Produce a VOICELESS PALATAL PLOSIVE, [c]. Say it on its own and between vowels.

Add voicing to produce a VOICED PALATAL PLOSIVE, [ɟ]. Alternate [caɟa], [ɟɛcɛ], etc.

Go back to the [k] position (voiced velar plosive). Now feel backwards and downwards with the back of the tongue, moving it down along the velum until the extreme back of the tongue articulates with the extreme end of the soft palate and the UVULA. Try to make a VOICELESS UVULAR PLOSIVE, [q]. Repeat it a few times and put it between vowels.

Add voicing to produce a VOICED UVULAR PLOSIVE, [ɢ]. Compare and contrast [c, ɟ], [k, g], [q, ɢ].

You should have no difficulty in producing a PALATAL NASAL [ɲ] or a UVULAR NASAL [N]. The first is articulated just like [ɟ], except that the soft palate is down; the second has the same relationship to [ɢ].

Keep the tip of your tongue out of the way for [ɲ]: compare it with the sequence [nj], as in English *onion*. Say the French word *montagne* [mɔ̃'taɲ].

If you can make a lateral at this place of articulation, it will be a
VOICED PALATAL LATERAL, [ʎ]. Note its articulation by the FRONT of
the tongue, as compared with the TIP (or BLADE) articulation for [lj]
as in English *million*.

Repeat the VELAR FRICATIVES [x, ɣ] learnt earlier. Now produce
PALATAL and UVULAR fricatives by moving the body of the tongue
forward and back, as just practised for the palatal and uvular
plosives. With the FRONT of the tongue raised close to the HARD
PALATE, make a VOICELESS PALATAL FRICATIVE [ç] (Chapter 23). Note
its relationship to Cardinal 1, [i̱]—how do they differ articulatorily?
Alternate [çi̱çi̱çi̱]. The VOICED PALATAL FRICATIVE [ʝ] is even more
similar to [i̱]. (In this book we use the symbol [ʝ] for the fricative,
to distinguish it clearly from the frictionless continuant or semi-
vowel [j]. The IPA alphabet uses [j] in both senses.)

Sliding the tongue back from [x] gives a VOICELESS UVULAR
FRICATIVE, [χ].

Glide from palatal through velar to uvular fricative, [ç—x—χ],
and back again. Note how the pitch changes from high (palatal) to
low (uvular).

Produce the voiced counterpart of [χ], the VOICED UVULAR FRICA-
TIVE [ʁ] (Chapter 22). The French *r* is one or other of these: try the
following French words—

route	[ʁut̪]
quatre	[kat̪χ]
le roi	[lə ˈʁwɑ]
lettre	[ˈlɛt̪χ]
arriver	[aʁiˈve]

Then try some German words with [ç] and [x] or [χ]—

nicht	[nɪçt]	
Achtung	[ˈaxtʊŋ]	
Milch	[mɪlç]	(clear [l]!)
Buch	[bux]	

Children with pronunciation difficulties (dyslalia) often replace
alveolar fricatives by palatal, velar, uvular, or other fricatives.
Practise and write down some examples of this, using appropriate
phonetic symbols.

2. MORE FRICATIVES

Make a voiceless alveolar lateral (Chapter 3) before and after
vowels, e.g. [ɛ̥ɛ], [ḁa], [ɔ̥ɔ]. Then add friction between the sides

of the tongue and the teeth. This gives a VOICELESS ALVEOLAR LATERAL FRICATIVE, [ɬ].

Say [ɛɬɛ], [aɬa], [ɔɬɔ], etc.

[ɬ] is the sound of Welsh *ll*. Pronounce *Llanelli* [ɬa'nɛɬi], *cyllell* ("knife") ['kəɬɛɬ], being careful to avoid the common English mistake of saying [θl] or [xl] instead of [ɬ].

Some people who lisp use [ɬ] for [s]. Pronounce some words lisping in this way—e.g. *see, six, voice, assist*.

Add voice to [ɬ] to get the VOICED ALVEOLAR LATERAL FRICATIVE, [ɮ]. Lisp by using it for [z] in words such as *easy, noises, zinc*.

Using the same kind of tongue position as was used for [ṭ, ḍ, ṇ], produce VOICELESS and VOICED RETROFLEX FRICATIVES, [ʂ] and [ʐ]. Practise them before and after vowels.

Compare [ʂ] and [ʐ] with the voiceless and voiced PALATO-ALVEOLAR fricatives, [ʃ] and [ʒ]. Note the difference in the pitch of resonance: [ʂ] has a lower pitch than [ʃ]. Slur from [ʂ] to [ʃ], listening to the gradual rise in the resonance of the friction.

Now try and continue this rise, while maintaining the production of a voiceless [ʃ]-type fricative. This should give a VOICELESS ALVEOLO-PALATAL FRICATIVE, [ɕ]. Slur back from [ɕ] through [ʃ] to [ʂ].

Make the voiced counterpart of [ɕ], symbol [ʑ]. Slur from [ʑ] through [ʒ] to [ʐ], and back again to [ʑ]. Practise [ɕ] and [ʑ] before and after vowels.

Note that these sounds may function as allophones of English /j/ after /t/ and /d/, as in *tune, educate*.

A voiceless glottal fricative, [h], is produced by passing a relatively large flow of air through the parted vocal folds. On the other hand, passing a large flow of air through vibrating vocal folds gives a VOICED GLOTTAL FRICATIVE, [ɦ]. Make this sound—be passionate, sigh as you speak.

Try the VOICELESS PHARYNGEAL FRICATIVE, [ħ]. This is articulated by a constriction in the pharynx, between the root of the tongue and the wall of the pharynx. Its voiced counterpart, [ʕ], is often accompanied by "creaky" voice.

3. MULTIPLE ARTICULATIONS

It is quite easy to pronounce [f] and [s] simultaneously. The resultant [f͡s] is said to have DOUBLE ARTICULATION—labiodental and alveolar. Plosives and nasals can be similarly double-articulated: e.g. [k͡p], [m͡ŋ]. In these cases the two places of articulation are of equal importance.

Sometimes, however, a sound-type with two places of articulation clearly has one of them more important, one less important. In the case of dark [ɫ], for example (Chapter 19), the alveolar articulation is PRIMARY, the velar articulation SECONDARY (Chapter 9). A secondary articulation is defined as one having a lesser DEGREE OF STRICTURE than a simultaneous primary articulation.

Secondary articulations are given names ending in -IZED and -IZATION. So the proper name for [ɫ] is a VELARIZED voiced alveolar lateral. The /t/ in *twin*, which has lip-rounding, [t̬], is a LABIALIZED voiceless alveolar plosive. A consonant with secondary palatal articulation is termed PALATALIZED, e.g. [t̬]—and so on.

4. SECONDARY CARDINAL VOWELS

Adding lip-rounding to cardinal vowels 1 to 5 gives the secondary cardinals 1 to 5, [y, ø, ,œ Œ, ɒ]. Spreading the lips while having the tongue position for cardinals 6 to 8 gives the secondary cardinals 6 to 8, [ʌ, ɤ, ɯ].

> Make [y] by rounding the lips while keeping the tongue position for [i]. Practise alternating [i—y—i—y], moving the lips only and keeping the tongue steady.
>
> Do similar exercises to derive [ø] from [e] and [œ] from [ɛ].
>
> Say French and German words with FRONT ROUNDED VOWELS of this type, e.g.
> [plym] *plume* "pen"
> [jø] *yeux* "eyes"
> [œf] *œuf* "egg";
> ['mydə] *müde* "tired"
> [ʃøn] *schön* "beautiful"
> ['ʔœfnən] *öffnen* "to open"
>
> Make [ɯ]—a CLOSE BACK UNROUNDED vowel—by saying cardinal [u] and then spreading the lips while keeping the same tongue position. Alternate [u—ɯ—u—ɯ—u], moving the lips only and keeping the tongue steady. Say some Japanese words: [mizɯ] "water," [sɯmɯ] "live," [ɸɯdʒi] "Fuji."

Ordinary [w] has double articulation, since it is a voiced frictionless continuant with both bilabial and velar articulations (for short, LABIO-VELAR semivowel). Just as [w] corresponds in articulation to [u], so the semivowel corresponding to [y] is [ɥ], the VOICED LABIO-PALATAL SEMIVOWEL (i.e. bilabial/palatal frictionless continuant).

> Say the French words
> [ɥit̬] *huit* "eight"
> [sɥi] *suis* "am"; and compare
> [lɥi] *lui* "him" with [lwi] *Louis*.

106

The voiceless counterpart of [w] which some people use for *wh*, [ʍ], may often have friction at the bilabial place but not at the velar, and thus be a voiceless velarized bilabial fricative.

EAR-TRAINING

Nonsense words

ˈløɟyq   pæˈɫœχ   ˈcɯxa̰j   weˈ̥ɖøsyɞ   qa̰ˈsyʧɔz

Try transcribing this passage of no known language from dictation—

ø ˈhy øˈjø, ɯ ˈcɑ ʐɒˈzœ.
yˈxɛ œʒy ˈnø sa ˈl̥øno, e ʀut yˈçɛn ˈzamɟɔm̩, yˈnœ ˈɖixɛ uˈcɯ a ˈɲaɪx.

Appendix 1   Some English Phonemes and their Allophones

This table is not exhaustive. In particular, it does not show GLOTTALIZATION, which may occur in certain of the syllable-final contexts marked [1] below, PALATALIZATION (before /j/), LABIALIZATION (for /r/ etc. and before /w, u/ etc.), or different APPROACH features of plosives. Nor is it possible to show the accumulation of special features in certain cases: e.g. the /t/ in *true* is commonly (i) post-alveolar, (ii) affricated, and (iii) labialized.

		Feature	*Context*	*Example*
/p/	Voicing:	voiceless	all	
	Place:	bilabial	all, except:	
		labiodental	before /f, v/	*cupful*
	Manner:	plosive	all	
	Aspiration:	aspirated [pʰ]	initial in stressed syllable	*park, appear*
		unaspirated [p⁼]	after /s/	*spark*
			medial, final[1,2,3]	*happy, cap*
	Release	oral	all, except:	
		nasal [pᵐ]	before nasal[1]	*topmost*
		non-audible [pᵀ]	before /t, d, k, g/[1,2]	*apt*
		none [p^]	before /p, b/[1]	*chipboard*
	Fortis/lenis:	fortis	all	
/t/	Voicing:	voiceless	all[4]	
	Place:	alveolar	all, except	
		dental [t̪]	before /θ, ð/[1,2]	*eighth, but then*
		post-alveolar [t̠]	before /r/[1]	*train, country*
		glottal [ʔ]	syllable-final[2]	*at large*
	Manner:	plosive	all	
	Aspiration:	aspirated [tʰ]	initial in stressed syllable	*team, attack*
		unaspirated [t⁼]	after /s/	*steam*
			medial, final[1,2,3]	*water, hot*
	Release:	oral	all, except:	
		nasal [tⁿ]	before nasal[1]	*chutney, button*
		lateral [tˡ]	before /l, ḷ/[1]	*Scotland, bottle*

[1,2,3,4]. For notes see page 111.

108

		non-audible [tˀ]	before /p, b, k, g/[1,2]	*outcome*
		none [tˆ]	before /t, d/[1]	*hot dog*
	Fortis/lenis:	fortis	all	

/d/	Voicing:	voiced	all, except:	
		partly or wholly voiceless [d̥]	next to fortis cons. or pause	*bedtime*
	Place:	alveolar	all, except:	
		dental [d̪]	before /θ, ð/[2]	*width, said that*
		post-alveolar [ḏ]	before /r/	*drain, sundry*
	Manner:	plosive	all	
	Release:	oral	all, except:	
		nasal [dⁿ]	before nasal	*midnight, sudden*
		lateral [dˡ]	before /l, ļ/	*sadly, saddle*
		non-audible [dˀ]	before /p, b, k, g/[2]	*broadcast*
		none [dˆ]	before /t, d/	*bedtime*
	Fortis/lenis:	lenis	all	

/n/	Voicing:	voiced	all, except:	
		partly voiceless [n̥]	after fortis cons.[2]	*snap*
	Place:	alveolar	all, except:	
		dental [n̪]	before /θ, ð/[2]	*tenth*
		post-alveolar [ṉ]	before /r, tr, dr/	*sunrise, laundry*
	Manner:	nasal	all	
	Fortis/lenis:	lenis	all	

(*Note:* /ņ/ is as /n/, but of longer duration.)

/g/	Voicing:	voiced	all, except:	
		partly or wholly voiceless [g̊]	next to fortis cons. or pause	*outgrow*
	Place:	velar	all, except:	
		pre-velar [g̟]	before front vowel or /j/	*geese*
		post-velar [ḡ]	before back vowel or /w/	*goose*
	Manner:	plosive	all	
	Release:	oral	all, except:	
		nasal [gᵑ]	before nasal	*ignore*
		non-audible [gˀ]	before /p, b, t, d/[2]	*lagged*
		none [gˆ]	before /k, g/	*big game*
	Fortis/lenis:	lenis	all	

/dʒ/ Voicing   voiced   all, except:

/dʒ/	Voicing	voiced	all, except:	
		partly or wholly voiceless [dʒ̥, d̥ʒ, d̥ʒ̥]	next to fortis cons. or pause	*large size*
	Place:	palato-alveolar	all	
	Manner:	affricate	all	
	Fortis/lenis:	lenis	all	

/z/	Voicing:	voiced	all, except:	
		partly or wholly voiceless [z̥]	next to fortis cons. or pause	*was called*
	Place:	alveolar	all	
	Manner:	fricative	all	
	Fortis/lenis:	lenis	all	

/r/	Voicing:	voiced	all, except:	
		partly or wholly voiceless [ɹ̥]	after fortis cons.	*train, cry*
	Place:	post-alveolar⁵	all	
	Manner:	frictionless continuant [ɹ]	all, except:	
		fricative [ɹ̝]	after /p, t, d, k/	*drink*
	Fortis/lenis:	lenis	all, except:	
		fortis	after /t/	*train*

/l/	Voicing:	voiced	all, except:	
		partly or wholly voiceless [l̥]	after /p, k/	*plane, clue*
	Place:	alveolar	all, except:	
		dental [l̪]	before /θ, ð/	*wealth*
		post-alveolar [l̠]	before /r, tr, dr/	*already, poultry*
	Manner:	lateral non-fricative	all (or some friction when voiceless)	
	Fortis/lenis:	lenis	all	

(*Note:* for velarization—dark [ɫ]—see Chapter 19.)

VOWELS (all are voiced and vocoid)

/u/	Place:	nearly back [ü]	all, except:	
		central [ʉ]	after /j/	*new*
		back [u]	before [ɫ]	*fool*
	Height:	close	all	
	Lips:	lightly rounded	all	

Duration:	relatively long [u:]	all, except:		
	shorter [u]		before fortis cons. in same syllable	*root*
			before unstressed syllable in same word	*ruder*
			unstressed	*unite*

/ə/	Place:	central	all	
	Height:	between half-close and half-open	all, except:	
		half-open	final	*sofa*
		half-close	before /k, g, ŋ/	*recognize*
	Lips:	unrounded	all	
	Duration:	relatively short	all	

/ɛ/	Place	front	all, except:	
		between front and central [ɛ̈]	before [ɫ]	*tell*
	Height:	between half-close and half-open	all	
	Lips:	unrounded	all	
	Duration:	relatively short	all	

---

[1] Possible glottalization.

[2] Depending on speaker or style of speech.

[3] Finally: free variation between aspirated and unaspirated.

[4] Some speakers voice /t/ intervocalically, [t̬], e.g. *better*.

[5] Some speakers use an alveolar tap [ɾ] between vowels and/or after /θ, ð/.

Appendix 2 Books for Further Reading

Gimson, A. C. *An Introduction to the Pronunciation of English*. London: Edward Arnold, 2nd edition, 1970.

Jones, Daniel. *The Pronunciation of English*. Cambridge University Press, 1966.

The above are the standard works on English phonetics. For general phonetics, consult

Abercrombie, D. *Elements of General Phonetics*. Edinburgh University Press, 1967.

And for English intonation

O'Connor, J. D., and Arnold, G. F. *Intonation of Colloquial English*. London: Longmans, 1961.

Halliday, M. A. K. *Intonation of British English*.

The standard English pronouncing dictionary (but note that it uses a different transcription from the one used in this book) is

Jones, Daniel, revised by A. C. Gimson. *Everyman's English Pronouncing Dictionary*. London: Dent, 1967.

See also

Miller, G. M., *BBC Pronouncing Dictionary of British Names*. London: Oxford University Press, 1971.

Index

Index of Phonetic Symbols

115